THE WORLD OF ANIMALS

an illustrated encyclopedia
for young readers

TORMONT

HOW TO USE THE ENCYCLOPEDIA

Using this encyclopedia is very simple. Just look for the topic that interests you in the **index** at the back of the book, then go to the listed page.

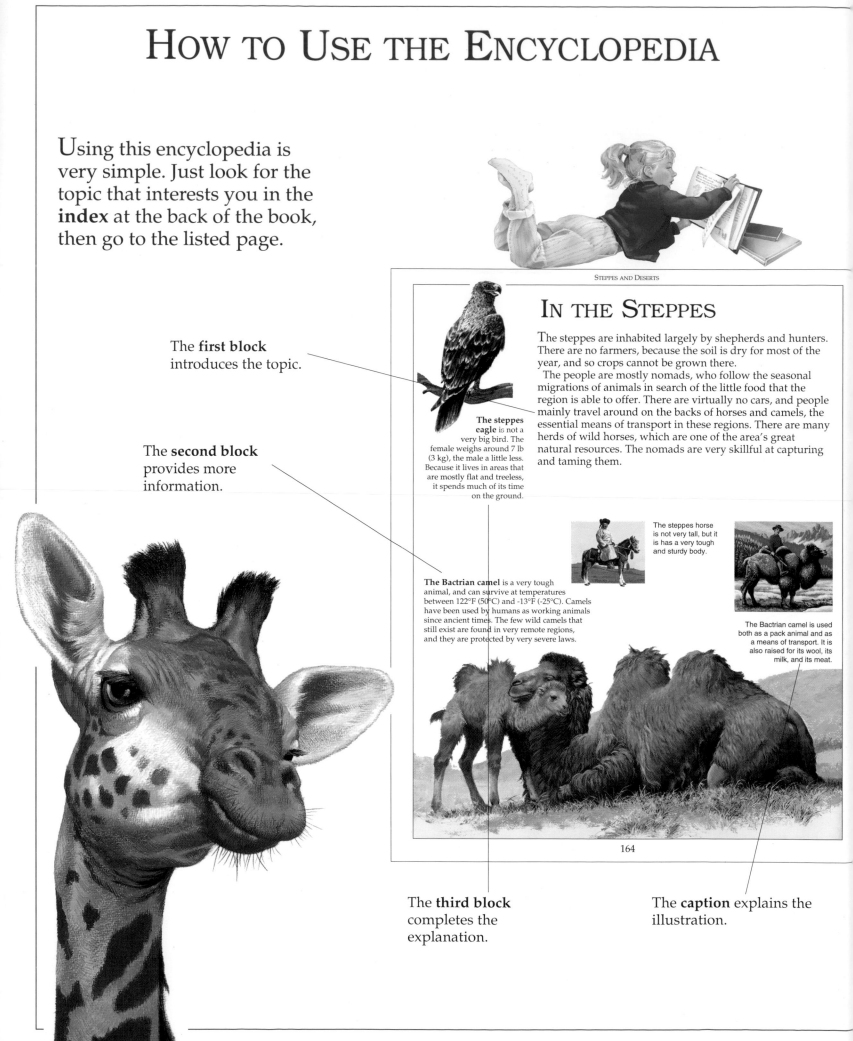

The **first block** introduces the topic.

The **second block** provides more information.

IN THE STEPPES

The steppes are inhabited largely by shepherds and hunters. There are no farmers, because the soil is dry for most of the year, and so crops cannot be grown there.

The people are mostly nomads, who follow the seasonal migrations of animals in search of the little food that the region is able to offer. There are virtually no cars, and people mainly travel around on the backs of horses and camels, the essential means of transport in these regions. There are many herds of wild horses, which are one of the area's great natural resources. The nomads are very skillful at capturing and taming them.

The steppes eagle is not a very big bird. The female weighs around 7 lb (3 kg), the male a little less. Because it lives in areas that are mostly flat and treeless, it spends much of its time on the ground.

The steppes horse is not very tall, but it is has a very tough and sturdy body.

The Bactrian camel is a very tough animal, and can survive at temperatures between 122°F (50°C) and -13°F (-25°C). Camels have been used by humans as working animals since ancient times. The few wild camels that still exist are found in very remote regions, and they are protected by very severe laws.

The Bactrian camel is used both as a pack animal and as a means of transport. It is also raised for its wool, its milk, and its meat.

164

The **third block** completes the explanation.

The **caption** explains the illustration.

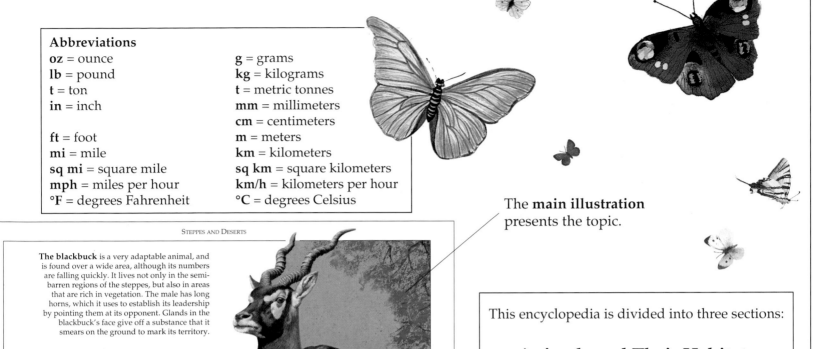

Abbreviations

oz = ounce	**g** = grams
lb = pound	**kg** = kilograms
t = ton	**t** = metric tonnes
in = inch	**mm** = millimeters
	cm = centimeters
ft = foot	**m** = meters
mi = mile	**km** = kilometers
sq mi = square mile	**sq km** = square kilometers
mph = miles per hour	**km/h** = kilometers per hour
°F = degrees Fahrenheit	**°C** = degrees Celsius

The **main illustration** presents the topic.

The blackbuck is a very adaptable animal, and is found over a wide area, although its numbers are falling quickly. It lives not only in the semi-barren regions of the steppes, but also in areas that are rich in vegetation. The male has long horns, which it uses to establish its leadership by pointing them at its opponent. Glands in the blackbuck's face give off a substance that it smears on the ground to mark its territory.

When in danger, the blackbuck flees by making long jumps. This escape tactic usually confuses the predator.

The onager is a wild donkey with a yellowish-brown coat. It spends much of the day looking for food, stopping every once in a while to roll in the dust in an effort to rid itself of parasites. At night, it rests on its side among the bushes.

The great bustard is a medium-sized bird that prefers to move by running along the ground, although it can fly perfectly well. It feeds on berries and seeds.

THE HIGHEST TEMPERATURE RECORDED IN THE SIBERIAN STEPPES IS 97°F (36°C). THE LOWEST RECORDED TEMPERATURE IS -90°F (-68°C).

165

The **box** highlights a special fact or concept.

Secondary illustrations highlight particular animals or interesting details.

This encyclopedia is divided into three sections:

Animals and Their Habitats
From POLAR REGIONS AND TUNDRA to THE FARMYARD, these are the eight main habitats where animals are found.

Classifications
The 'identity cards,' or scientific classifications of 546 animals, organized by the continent where each is found—plus domesticated animals.

Dictionaries
Dictionary of Fish,
Dictionary of Birds,
Dictionary of Reptiles and Amphibians,
Dictionary of Insects,
Dictionary of Ecology,
Dictionary of Famous Animals

Table of Contents

NATURAL HABITATS

The main habitats and the animals that live in them.

POLAR REGIONS AND TUNDRA
pages 13 to 40

STEPPES AND DESERTS
pages 161 to 182

MOUNTAINS
pages 41 to 68

TROPICAL FORESTS
pages 183 to 224

TEMPERATE FORESTS
pages 69 to 110

THE OCEANS
pages 225 to 256

GRASSLANDS AND SAVANNAHS
pages 111 to 160

FARMYARD AND DOMESTIC ANIMALS
pages 257 to 282

CLASSIFICATIONS

The class, order, family, genus, and species of animals from around the world.

ANIMALS OF THE AMERICAS
pages 284 to 289

ANIMALS OF AUSTRALIA, OCEANIA AND ANTARCTICA
pages 304 to 307

ANIMALS OF EUROPE
pages 290 to 294

DOMESTIC AND FARM ANIMALS
pages 308 to 310

ANIMALS OF ASIA
pages 295 to 299

ANIMALS OF AFRICA
pages 300 to 303

DICTIONARIES

Dictionary of Fish
pages 312 to 325

Dictionary of Insects
pages 344 to 351

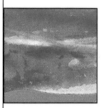

Dictionary of Birds
pages 326 to 337

Dictionary of Ecology
pages 352 to 359

Dictionary of Reptiles and Amphibians
pages 338 to 343

Dictionary of Famous Animals
pages 360 to 368

INDEX
pages 369 to 380

Polar Regions and Tundra

LIVING IN THE COLD

It does not seem possible that animals can live and reproduce in regions where the temperature is nearly always below the freezing point (32°F or 0°C). But even the coldest and least hospitable regions on Earth are inhabited. Some animals have developed ways to limit their loss of body heat. Penguins, for example, have a thick sub-layer of warm feathers beneath their top feathers, while polar bears are covered with thick, waterproof fur. All animals living in polar regions have a thick underlayer of fat to keep them warm.

Whereas seals live in both the Arctic and Antarctic regions, polar bears live only in Arctic regions. Many species of penguin live in Antarctica and in the cold oceans of the southern hemisphere.

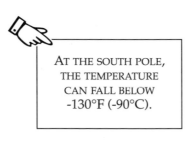

Accidental Migrations
Sometimes polar bears become stranded on icebergs, which are huge blocks of ice that drift out to sea. The bear then must swim a long way to return home.

AT THE SOUTH POLE, THE TEMPERATURE CAN FALL BELOW -130°F (-90°C).

Imitating animals – In order to survive the cold, people who live in polar regions imitate the way animals keep themselves warm. They do so by dressing in thick furs and sometimes they even smear whale fat on their bodies to keep warm.

The Arctic Ocean – Covering an area of about 5 million sq mi (14 million sq km), the Arctic Ocean can be as much as 11,500 ft (3,500 m) deep. Its permanently frozen waters cover the North Pole. There is no land here, only water and ice. The animals that live in the region, such as the walrus, are all excellent swimmers.

People everywhere build their homes with the materials easily available to them. In the Arctic, the native people, called Inuit, traditionally built dome-shaped temporary winter homes called igloos, using blocks of wind-compressed snow.

Tundra – This Arctic region is covered with snow for most of the year. When the snow melts, lichen and mosses appear, providing food for herbivores (plant-eating animals) such as the musk ox. Beneath this layer of plants is soil that is always frozen, called permafrost.

Antarctica – Unlike the North Pole, Antarctica is formed from land covered with ice. For this reason, it is known as the sixth continent. It's fauna (animal population) lives mainly along the coasts. Here, the key to life is the ocean, which provides abundant food for these animals in the form of plankton and tiny shrimp-like crustaceans called krill. Animals common to this region of the world include penguins, seals and elephant seals, albatrosses and petrels, killer whales or orcas, and other whales.

THE ARCTIC

The Arctic is the vast region surrounding the North Pole. It is mostly covered with pack ice, which is a massive sheet of ice that floats on the surface of the ocean. The Arctic also includes some areas of land, such as the northern coasts of Canada, the Scandinavian peninsula, Siberia, and most of Greenland. The average temperature is about -22°F (-30°C). Rain and snow are rare. The region was first explored in the late 16th century. The first explorer to reach the North Pole by surface travel was the American R. E. Peary, in 1909.

Native peoples – The Arctic regions of Greenland, Canada, Alaska, and eastern Siberia are populated by about one-hundred thousand native people, or Inuit (also called the Eskimo). Northern Europe is populated by the Sami (also called Laplanders), and Siberia by, among others, the Chukchi and Yakut.

1. fulmar

2. and **3.** puffin

4. snowy owl

5. reindeer

6. narwhal

7. lemming

8. common seal

9. arctic tern

10. polar bear

11. walrus

THE POLAR BEAR

In order to catch seals, on which it loves to feed, the polar bear will often stand for hours peering into a hole in the ice. When a seal surfaces to breathe, the bear snatches it and drags it out of the water.

Newborn polar bear cubs are tiny, blind, deaf, and helpless. Because of this, they stay with their mothers for up to two years before venturing out into the world. Their thick, waterproof fur is pure white, providing a perfect camouflage against the whiteness of their icy world. They are excellent swimmers, with 'fingers' and toes that are joined by a membrane that helps them to swim. The polar bear is the world's largest carnivore (meat-eater).

Weight – Polar bears usually weigh between 330 and 1,100 lb (150 to 500 kg), although some have weighed over 1,540 lb (700 kg).

The Arctic Circle is located at the 66th parallel. From this parallel to the North Pole, there is at least 1 full 24-hour day of

sunlight in the summer, and a 24-hour period of darkness in winter.

During the short summer, many types of whales migrate to the Arctic seas. In the winter months, whales generally return south to mate.

Arctic terns are like gulls, in that they often follow ships, and wait for the garbage thrown overboard by sailors.

POLAR BEARS CAN LIVE FOR UP TO THIRTY YEARS.

This sea otter is swimming with its baby on its chest. Sea otters are often prey to polar bears.

Polar bear cubs – In late fall, female polar bears move inland to dig a den in the snow. Cubs are born in December or January, usually in pairs. They will not leave the den until the spring.

SEALS AND SEA LIONS

Along the cold coastlines and on the vast ice floes of the Arctic there live many species of pinnipeds (animals with flippers), including sea lions, seals, and walruses. Seals move on land by dragging themselves along on their stomachs, while sea lions can partially raise themselves up onto their front limbs, which have gradually evolved into flippers. Originally terrestrial (land-based), these animals have made a successful transition to life in the water. Their bodies have adapted to the marine environment. Unlike cetaceans (whales, dolphins, and porpoises), however, pinnipeds have adapted only partially, in that they must still return to land to give birth to their young.

Hunting for fish
Albatrosses, gulls, and pelicans often follow seals that are hunting, because fish startled by the seals often rise to the surface where the birds can easily snap them up.

Pinnipeds have large nostrils, through which they can breathe air very quickly. This allows them to spend very little time at the surface while they hunt for food underwater, or escape their enemies.

Periods of inactivity – Pinnipeds feed not just on fish, but also on shellfish, mollusks, and krill. When their stomachs are full after a successful hunting expedition, both seals and sea lions leave the water and lie for hours in the sun, occasionally rolling lazily around on the shore. Sometimes a killer whale will lunge from the sea and snatch away the closest animal.

Northern fur seal – Although similar to the sea lion, the northern fur seal has a thicker coat and a shorter, more pointed muzzle. The male can weigh up to four times more than the female. During the breeding season, the male goes in search of the breeding site. The female follows later, and eventually gives birth to just one cub.

The only pinniped that lives in warm waters is the monk seal, which is found in the Mediterranean, the Caribbean, and the waters around Hawaii. It is also thought to be in danger of becoming extinct.

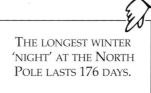

THE LONGEST WINTER 'NIGHT' AT THE NORTH POLE LASTS 176 DAYS.

WALRUS

This long-tusked mammal inhabits the seas of the high Arctic and will make brief seasonal migrations. Male walruses are enormous, and weigh up to 3,300 lb (1,500 kg). Females generally weigh less than 2,200 lb (1,000 kg). The walrus's heavy body is covered with wrinkles and a few bristly hairs. Its powerful call sounds like a cross between the roar of a lion and the bellow of a bull. While it is sleeping, whether on the ice or in the sea, it snores loudly. Walruses are quick-tempered and irritable, but will not move in to help if another walrus is being attacked by hunters. They spend long periods of time lazing in the sun.

Fat – Beneath its skin, the walrus has a thick layer of fat, which offers protection against the cold and also serves as a reserve energy supply when its food— mollusks, shrimp and occasionally small seals or dead whale meat—is scarce.

Tusks – The long tusks of this massive animal are essential to its survival. Walruses use their tusks as defensive weapons, for dredging the sea bed, as levers for hauling themselves up on to the shore or ice, and as an aid in moving along on ice and land. At one time, walrus tusks were much sought after as a material for making ornamental objects.

A young walrus is nursed by its mother for about two years, and then remains under her protection for a further two years.

Crowded beaches

Because of their great size and because their limbs are not well adapted for walking, walruses find it hard to move on land. After coming out of the water, they doze in the sun in tightly packed colonies, occupying all the available space. They often quarrel with each other to win a particular spot on the beach. The stronger animals eventually chase away those that are less aggressive.

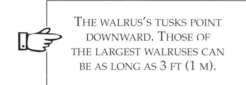

THE WALRUS'S TUSKS POINT DOWNWARD. THOSE OF THE LARGEST WALRUSES CAN BE AS LONG AS 3 FT (1 M).

Fierce battles – These slow, lazy-looking animals often engage in brief fights, raising their heads in a threatening manner, pointing their tusks at their opponents and letting out loud roars. They rarely hurt each other.

ARCTIC BIRDS

Northern regions are home to a large number of birds, all of which are migratory. The birds catch their food from the sea, which provides an endless supply of food for so many animals. The birds arrive in the region at the end of the long arctic night, which continues for the whole winter and part of the spring. In early fall, they fly south again.

Because puffins can carry several fish in their mouths at one time, they do not need to keep returning to shore while out fishing.

Around mid-March, puffins gather in large colonies to search the ground for a good nesting site.

Underground nests
Nesting pairs of puffins use their beaks and claws to dig into the earth, creating a long underground tunnel that ends with a chamber in which the female lays a single egg. Sometimes other animals, such as rabbits, try to take over the nest.

The arctic tern often nests on uninhabited islands far from the coast, and is usually found far out at sea. It migrates over very long distances, often traveling tens of thousands of miles (kilometers). We still do not know why it makes such long journeys.

The razorbill is a medium-size bird, about 16 in (40 cm) long. It has a powerful black beak with a white band, and nests in ravines and caves along the cliffs of the Atlantic coastline.

A PUFFIN CAN HOLD AS MANY AS 20 FISH IN ITS BEAK, CARRYING THEM SIDEWAYS AS IF ITS BEAK WERE A SKEWER

Snowy owl – A stealthy nocturnal hunter, the snowy owl is a constant threat to the young of other birds still in the nest. It also feeds on small rodents like mice and lemmings.

The female razorbill usually lays two eggs. Both parents take care of the fledglings.

25

ANTARCTICA

Land and ice – Ninety-eight percent of the continent of Antarctica is covered with ice. Because there are no warm sea currents, Antarctica is much colder than Arctic regions. Temperatures never rise above 32°F (0°C). There are no permanent human settlements, but there are many scientific research stations, both inland and along the coasts. Even in this inhospitable part of the world, many animals have adapted in order to survive and reproduce.

Exploration – The first person to reach the South Pole was the Norwegian explorer Roald Amundsen, in 1911.

Volcanoes and icebergs
The highest summit in Antarctica is the active volcano Erebus (12,444 ft/3,794 m). The icebergs from Antarctica are often huge floating ice mountains, which are formed when the icecap extends over the landmass and breaks off into the sea. In contrast, arctic icebergs tend to be wide, fairly flat tables of ice.

1. albatross
2. leopard seal
3. blue whale
4. elephant seal
5. Gentoo penguin
6. king penguin
7. rockhopper penguin
8. sea lion

THE TUNDRA

Harsh environment – The tundra region is found close to the Arctic Circle. Tundra vegetation includes mosses, lichen, hardy grasses and shrubs—but no tall trees. Much of this region has *permafrost* (permanently frozen ground) just beneath the ground surface which prevents the growth of plants with deep roots.

Migrations – In the spring when the plants begin to grow, birds, rodents, and carnivores (meat-eaters) migrate to the region where food is plentiful.

Few human beings – Because the tundra cannot sustain agriculture, very few people live there, those that do will often stay for only a few months each year.

1. **long-tailed jaeger**
2. **snowy owl**
3. **ptarmigan**
4. **caribou**
5. **arctic wolf**
6. **arctic fox**
7. **musk ox**
8. **Canada goose**
9. **red-breasted merganser**
10. **arctic loon**
11. **arctic hare**
12. **lemming**
13. **snow bunting**
14. **oldsquaw**
15. **grayling**

MUSK OX

The musk ox has round, strong horns that initially grow straight and flat, but then curve sharply upward. The horns are also present in the female.

In the northernmost regions of the American continent—in Canada, Alaska, and Greenland—lives the musk ox. With its broad horns and long shaggy coat, it is well adapted to life in the harsh climate of this region. Musk oxen live in small herds, feeding on the sparse arctic vegetation, which includes mosses, lichen, and shrubs. Their natural enemies are bears and wolves. They are aggressive animals, and frequently engage in fierce battles among themselves.

Defense – When under attack by wolves, musk oxen huddle together in a circle, facing outward toward their enemy, with their young protected at the center of the herd.

Calves – The female musk ox normally produces one calf every two years.

32

LEMMINGS AND GROUND SQUIRRELS

Lemmings and ground squirrels are both small rodents. It is a myth that lemmings control their population by killing themselves in large groups—thought to be by running off cliffs into rivers or the sea. In reality, however, many lemmings often die during their spring migrations while trying to swim across large rivers. Lemmings breed very quickly, and those that remain soon restore their original numbers.

Lemmings do not hibernate. They dig underground burrows, which they stock with food supplies.

Lemming – The lemming is the most common small rodent in the northern regions of the world. It feeds on seeds, leaves, shoots, and other vegetation.

THE FRONT TEETH OF A RODENT KEEP GROWING THROUGHOUT ITS LIFE.

The ground squirrel looks like a marmot, but is smaller (around 9 in/22 cm long). In Russia, populations of the souslik, a European ground squirrel, often grow so large that they pose a problem for farm production, and each year destroy millions of tons of crops.

ARCTIC WOLF

The color of the arctic wolf's coat matches its surrounding habitat, providing camouflage against the whiteness of the snow. The wolf pack is therefore able to creep up on its prey without being seen. The arctic wolf generally preys on large herbivores (grass-eating animals) such as musk oxen and elk. It also attacks other, smaller animals, such as beavers, rabbits, ground squirrels, and mice.

A she-wolf gives birth to five or six cubs, which she looks after for only two months.

Wolves follow herds of caribou and reindeer, traveling up to 60 mi (100 km) in one day.

A WOLF CAN DEVOUR AS MUCH AS 22 LB (10 KG) OF MEAT A DAY.

SLED DOGS

In cold, polar regions, people traditionally used sled dogs to help them move around. The breeds best suited to this work are the husky and the Alaskan malamute. Tireless and strong, these animals can withstand polar temperatures and do not need large amounts of food. Although nowadays people generally travel around on snowmobiles, sled dogs are still used for recreation and sporting competitions.

The number of dogs in a team varies according to the weight of the sled.

Huskies are proud animals and are not very sociable with one another or playful with humans. But they are very faithful to their owners.

The Gold Rush – In the late 1800s, large gold deposits were discovered in Alaska and the Yukon. Huskies were of great help to transport the miners and their equipment to remote mining regions.

Sense of direction – Even during snowstorms, huskies have an amazing sense of direction which enables them to find their way home.

Wolves – Huskies and malamutes are direct descendants of wolves, and can still interbreed with them.

BIRDS OF THE TUNDRA

The long-tailed jaeger nests in Arctic regions and then migrates to Antarctica, covering enormous distances.

Large numbers of birds fly to these barren regions in the spring, feeding mostly on shoots, berries, fish, or small mammals such as lemmings and ground squirrels. As with all cold regions, most of the birds fly south in the fall when food supplies become scarce.

Hunting – With its sharp eyesight, the snowy owl is able to hunt for small rodents even in poor light.

Camouflage – Many tundra birds change the color of their plumage in order to adapt to the color of their surrounding habitat and so hide from predators.

The snow geese shown here are in their white plumage, but they can also be grayish-blue in color. Snow geese move in large flocks, stopping to feed around riverbanks and marshlands.

REINDEER

In Scandinavian countries the reindeer is a very popular animal, and legend has it that a team of reindeer pulls Santa Claus' sleigh across the sky. Wild reindeer migrate in search of regions with plentiful food. During these migrations, females and calves travel ahead of the males, which follow a few days behind. Both males and females have antlers. North American reindeer are called caribou.

The reindeer's antlers fall off once a year, but begin to grow again immediately.

Searching for food

In the winter, the reindeer digs down through the deep snow with its hooves to find grass to eat.

THE ANTLERS OF THE REINDEER CAN GROW AS LONG AS 60 IN (150 CM).

Arctic Fox

The arctic fox is found only in Arctic regions. There are two main types of arctic fox: the white fox and the blue fox. With its white fur and black-tipped tail, the white fox is perfectly camouflaged during the winter months. In the summer, when there is little or no snow, its fur darkens to brown. The blue fox, which lives in areas where there is little or no snow (in the Aleutian and Pribilof Islands, for example), is gray-blue in summer and lighter in winter.

Foxes do not live in packs. They are solitary animals that dig burrows in the dry earth.

Red fox – This close relative of the arctic fox is found virtually all over the world.

Large and small – Species of arctic fox that live on islands are found to be slightly smaller than those living on the mainland.

Eating habits – The arctic fox is a member of the canine (dog) family. It is very adaptable and can vary its diet without difficulty. Although it feeds mostly on small rodents and hares, or on eggs that it finds in nests, it will also eat fish and animal carcasses tossed ashore by the sea. During the winter, arctic foxes follow bears, feeding on their leftovers.

SAIGA

Only the male saiga has horns, which grow to a length of around 12 in (30 cm).

The saiga is a type of wild sheep that lives in the tundra of Central Asia. Like many other grass-eating animals, such as deer, camels, and cows, the saiga is a ruminant, which means that it has a four-chambered stomach adapted to digest grass, and it chews its cud. Although it has a long, highly flexible, almost trunk-like nose, the saiga's sense of smell (like its sense of hearing) is rather poor. It has very good eyesight, however. Saigas generally live in small herds, but when food becomes scarce they gather in herds of thousands of animals, migrating long distances in search of a more hospitable habitat. The saiga was hunted for centuries, but has been a protected species for around eighty years.

The stomach of a ruminant is divided into four parts:
1. rumen   **2.** reticulum
3. omasum   **4.** abomasum

Hidden in the grass – The female saiga normally gives birth to two young, which she nurses for around two months. While they are small, the young saiga stay in grassy areas, hidden from predators.

ERMINE AND MINK

The tail of the ermine—once the prized fur of kings.

The ermine and the mink, like the weasel, belong to the mustelid family, a group of small carnivores with long bodies, sleek fur, small legs, and sharp claws. Their fur, like that of many other mammals, has two layers: an under layer of downy fur and a top layer of longer hairs. They are skillful hunters, feeding on small rodents, such as mice.

Ermine – At around 14 in (35 cm) long, the ermine is smaller than the mink. It lives in the cold regions of North America, Europe, and Asia, as well as in other habitats. It can also be found on the slopes of the Caucasus Mountains and in the mountains of Algeria. It is a solitary animal that hunts by night.

Mink – Also known as the lutreola, the mink can reach a length of 24 in (60 cm), including its 6 in (15 cm) tail. It lives alone near streams and beaver ponds, and feeds on frogs, freshwater mollusks, and crustaceans. Minks are native to North America, Europe, and Asia, though they are now raised in many countries for their prized fur.

Changing colors – During the winter, the mink's brown fur becomes as white as the snow in which it hides. The end of its tail, however, remains black.

Mountains

LIFE IN THE MOUNTAINS

Few people live in high mountain regions. The land is often very difficult to cultivate, or it is used by humans only in the summer as pasture for farm animals. For the last hundred years or so, mountainous areas have also become used for pleasure and recreation, first for mountaineering, and more recently for skiing. The building of roads, ski-lifts, hotels, and homes for winter vacationers often causes harm to the natural environment and beauty of these regions.

A young chamois peers intently at the land around him.

Beautiful flowers, such as the columbine, grow in the high mountain areas, even where the terrain is very rocky.

Ecology – The growing number of people who enjoy visiting mountain regions around the world has brought economic growth to local communities. Unfortunately, it has also increased the impact of humans on the delicate natural balance in these environments.

Vicuña – This relative of the camel is found in the Andes Mountains of South America. Vicuñas live either in family groups that include males, females, and young, or in all-male herds. Once hunted for their extremely soft fur, they are now subject to very strict protection laws.

The langur is a monkey that is almost entirely vegetarian and lives in the mountains of Asia.

THE WORLD'S HIGHEST CAPITAL CITY IS LHASA, TIBET, WHICH STANDS AT 11,900 FT (3,630 M).

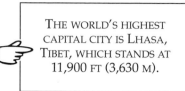

Capercaillie – This colorful bird lives in the mountain forests of Europe and Asia. During the winter it lives among the branches of evergreen trees, feeding on the juiciest young needles. In summer, when the snow is gone, it rummages about on the ground in search of seeds and shoots.

THE MOUNTAINS OF NORTH AMERICA

The Rocky Mountains
Located in the western part of North America, the Rocky Mountains are around 3,100 mi (5,000 km) long, running north-south from Alaska to New Mexico. The terrain and climate do not generally favor either agriculture or the summer pasturing of sheep and cattle at higher elevations, so this is restricted to only a few valleys.

National Parks – The mountain landscape is so extraordinarily beautiful that the governments of Canada and the United States have created a number of very large and famous national parks in the region, including Canada's Banff and Jasper parks and the Yellowstone, Glacier, Grand Teton, and Rocky Mountain parks in the United States.

1. **Rocky Mountain goat**
2. **raven**
3. **golden eagle**
4. **pika, or 'calling hare'**
5. **yellowbelly marmot**
6. **grizzly bear**
7. **white sheep**
8. **wolverine**
9. **willow ptarmigan**

NORTH AMERICA

The large bighorn sheep has a brown coat and large curled horns.

During the last ice age—the long period of intense cold about 15,000 years ago when ice covered much of the Northern Hemisphere—the animals moved south in search of warmer climates. In Europe, as the animals moved south they came upon mountain barriers running from east to west. Those animals that were unable to cross the barriers died out and became extinct. In North America, however, the mountains run from north to south. Because of this, a larger number of species survived.

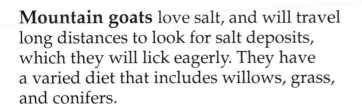

Mountain goats love salt, and will travel long distances to look for salt deposits, which they will lick eagerly. They have a varied diet that includes willows, grass, and conifers.

Grizzly bear – Once very common throughout the Rocky Mountains, the grizzly bear is now found only in the mountains of Canada and Alaska.

Dueling males – In mating season, bighorn sheep butt heads with each other so loudly that they can be heard from a great distance.

THE HIGHEST SUMMIT IN NORTH AMERICA IS ALASKA'S MOUNT McKINLEY (20,316 FT/6,194 M).

The wolverine is an inhabitant of the northern forests and looks like a small bear. It lives alone, digging a fresh burrow every night. This carnivore moves with a trotting or cantering motion. Because it attacks its victims in the open, they often manage to escape. The wolverine also eats animals killed by bears or mountain lions (pumas).

THE ANDES

The Cordilleras is the chain of mountain ranges extending from Alaska to the southern-most tip of South America. In the western part of South America lies the world's longest mountain range: the Andes cordillera. Running north-south, the cordillera is a succession of extremely high mountains, the highest of which is the volcano Mount Aconcagua (22,825 ft/6,959 m), Argentina.

Condor – The condor is one of the most spectacular birds in the Andes, with a wingspan of around 10 ft (over 3 m).

Llama – People in the Andes raise llamas for fur, leather, meat, and milk. Llamas are also used as pack animals.

1. **condor**
2. **puma or mountain lion**
3. **Magellan goose**
4. **vampire bat**
5. **guanaco**
6. **llama**
7. **alpaca**
8. **vicuña**
9. **pudu**
10. **magnificent hummingbird**
11. **red-tailed comet**
12. **brown-nosed coati**
13. **mountain viscacha**
14. **chinchilla**

SOUTH AMERICA

The mountains of the Andes cordillera are extremely high and steep, and the tops of most of them are covered in snow all year round. It is only in the milder climate of the northern Andes that one finds mountain plateaus inhabited and cultivated by humans. The Andes were formed relatively recently, in geological terms, having been pushed up from the depths of the oceans following a period of great geological upheaval. Because of this, they still include a number of active volcanoes, such as the Ojos del Salado (22,511 ft/6,863 m).

The paca is a nocturnal animal. A skillful swimmer, it lives close to streams and rivers.

Spectacled bear – This small black bear takes its name from the yellowish markings around its eyes. It lives in the northern mountains of the Andes.

THE ANDEAN CONDOR IS THE HEAVIEST OF ALL BIRDS OF PREY, WEIGHING UP TO 26 LB (12 KG).

Condor – One of the great birds of prey, the condor is found at a wide range of altitudes—from sea level to around 16,000 ft (5,000 m). Like other vultures, it lives together with others of its kind, unlike the solitary eagle, another well-known bird of prey.

Llama

These domesticated animals have been the pride of the Andes region since the time of the Incas, whose civilization flourished around the middle of the 15th century. The llama's fur, which is ideal for the region's severe climate, is thick and very soft. When frightened, llamas defend themselves in a very unusual way—they surprise and scare off their opponents by spitting forcefully at them!

The llama is related to the camel, but is smaller and has no humps.

The guanaco is the wild ancestor of the llama and the alpaca, and is also the largest mammal in South America, weighing up to 165 lb (75 kg). Once very common, it was hunted for its fur. It is now a protected species.

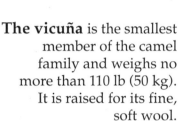

The vicuña is the smallest member of the camel family and weighs no more than 110 lb (50 kg). It is raised for its fine, soft wool.

The alpaca is raised mainly for its fine wool.

THE MOUNTAINS OF ASIA

The World's Highest Peak

The Himalayas, a range of mountains 2,018 mi (3,250 km) long, separates India from Central Asia. This range includes Mount Everest, which at 29,021 ft (8,848 m) is the tallest mountain in the world. It is named after George Everest, the nineteenth-century English topographer who was the first person to measure the mountain's height.

Diverse mountain habitats – Asia has more mountain ranges than any other continent, and its mountains span several latitudes. Because of this, the fauna also varies greatly, according to each region's climate and habitat. Whereas the high mountains and plateaus of Tibet are home to animals like the yak, which is perfectly adapted to the freezing climate, animals such as the panda prefer forested mountain regions with less severe temperatures. This illustration therefore shows the various animals—not that they necessarily live in the same regions.

1. **lesser, or red panda**
2. **bearded vulture**
3. **nilgai**
4. **takin**
5. **yak**
6. **tahr**
7. **argali**
8. **giant panda**
9. **four-horned antelope**
10. **Persian gazelle**
11. **musang**
12. **snow leopard**
13. **Asiatic black bear**

THE ROOF OF THE WORLD

Bam-i dunya, or the 'roof of the world,' is the name given by the local population to the Pamir Plateau, which stretches for 38,600 sq mi (100,000 sq km) across Tajikistan, Afghanistan, and China. The plateau has an average altitude of over 9,800 ft (3,000 m) and is surrounded by extremely high mountain ranges. With its sparse vegetation, its few streams and rivers, and its numerous lakes, it is a typical steppe-type environment.

The markhor has long, twisted horns.

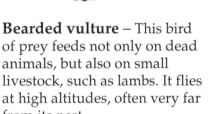

The pika is also known as the 'calling hare.'

Bearded vulture – This bird of prey feeds not only on dead animals, but also on small livestock, such as lambs. It flies at high altitudes, often very far from its nest.

Asiatic black bear – The fur of this bear is mostly black, but it also has white markings that resemble a collar on its chest. It feeds on vegetables, berries, and fruit, as well as on small river crustaceans and shellfish. It lives in forested areas and is a skillful tree climber.

The four-horned antelope is about the same size as a gazelle. The male has four horns (the front two horns are very short), while the female has none. They live in pairs or alone in the mountain forests of India, close to rivers and streams.

The langur's head is surrounded by a layer of thick fur that looks like a helmet.

Lady Amherst pheasant – With its brightly colored plumage and its long tail, this pheasant is found in mountain regions at elevations of about 6,500-9,800 ft (2,000-3,000 m). It lives in bamboo forests, feeding on bamboo shoots.

Musk deer – This unusual member of the cervidae family—which includes deer, moose, and elk—has no horns, but has highly developed upper canine teeth, or tusks, like those of carnivores. It is found from Tibet to Siberia, on the steepest mountains as well as in heavily wooded regions. The male has a gland called a musk bag, which secretes a very intense odor. This scent is used to make perfumes.

THE WORLD'S HIGHEST SUMMIT IS MOUNT EVEREST (29,021 FT / 8,848 M).

TAKIN AND YAK

Young takin are born after a gestation period of 8 months.

Similar to the domesticated ox, the takin is solidly built and awkward-looking, but is well adapted to living at altitudes between 8,000 and 13,000 ft (2,500 and 4,000 m). It is only during the winter, when food becomes scarce, that it heads down to lower-lying areas. Yaks live at even higher altitudes, up to 19,600 ft (6,000 m). They have been bred as pack animals by people for so many centuries that there are virtually no wild yaks remaining.

Takin – When startled by an aggressor, the takin hides in the thick of the forest and lies on the ground with its head down. It is so certain of not being seen that it can be approached without fear.

The yak's extremely thick, dark fur offers protection from the cold temperatures of the high mountains. Yaks are used for transporting people and goods at high altitudes.

THE LONGEST HIMALAYAN GLACIER IS THE SIACHEN GLACIER (47 MI/75.5 KM).

SNOW LEOPARD

Over 6.5 ft (2 m) long, including its tail, the snow leopard has thick fur and broad paws that prevent it from sinking into the snow. The coloring of its fur provides camouflage in its rocky habitat. An extremely agile animal, the snow leopard can easily hunt its prey in mountain areas. It is the only member of the cat family that jumps large distances, sometimes up to 50 ft (15 m). Although it used to be hunted for its fur, it is now a protected species.

One of the animals upon which the snow leopard preys is the Tibetan antelope, or chiru, which lives at altitudes of up to 16,400 ft (5,000 m).

Staying close to mother – The female snow leopard generally gives birth to two cubs. After they are weaned, the cubs go hunting with their mother, who takes up a position on high ground so that she has a clear view of the surrounding area. During the summer the snow leopard lives at very high altitudes, but in winter it heads down into the mountain valleys.

PANDA

The giant panda, with its distinctive face markings, is the symbol of the World Wildlife Fund (WWF), an international organization for the protection of nature and wildlife. The panda is now found only in the mountains of southwestern China and eastern Tibet, and at one time, it almost became extinct. The giant panda is now a protected species.

There are thought to be only a few hundred giant pandas left in the world.

The lesser, or red, panda is not as well-known as the giant panda. Its fur and long, ringed tail are reddish in color, and its legs and stomach are black.

Feeding habits – The giant panda is almost completely vegetarian. It eats mostly bamboo shoots, but also feeds on leaves, roots, flowers, and sometimes small rodents.

NEWBORN GIANT PANDA CUBS ARE AROUND 4 IN (10 CM) LONG.

Argali, Tahr and Markhor

At the roof of the world there live a number of goat-like herbivores with large horns. These animals are extremely agile, and are able to move quickly among steep rocks and graze in areas which are inaccessible to most other creatures. Some species, such as the tahr, are threatened with extinction even though they have few natural predators, apart from humans.

Argali – Also known as wild Altai sheep, the argali live in groups. The males have strong, well-developed horns and they sometimes engage in fierce fights, during which they butt each other violently, although they never seriously hurt one other.

The tahr can jump from a height of around 33 ft (10 m) without hurting itself. It has been successfully introduced into America.

A markhor pictured with its young.

The markhor has strange horns that twist vertically. It is even able to clamber along lower tree branches to feed on leaves and green twigs.

THE ALPS

The Alps include many of the highest mountains in Europe. In the shape of an arc, this mountain range extends about 680 miles (1,100 km) from east to west, and is never wider than 155 mi (250 km). The Alps cross a number of countries, including Italy, France, Switzerland, and Austria. Many summits are covered with snow all year round, and produce long rivers of ice, called glaciers.

The flora (plant life) is extremely varied, ranging from deciduous forests (with trees that shed their leaves each year) to coniferous forests. At around 6,500 ft (2,000 m), the trees give way to scrub land and meadows—this is known as the tree line or timberline.

The fauna (animal life) is also extremely varied, and flourishes despite the increasing presence of humans. The lynx, for example, was recently sighted in Italy for the first time in about two hundred years.

1. **golden eagle**
2. **deer**
3. **rock ptarmigan**
4. **black grouse**
5. **capercaillie**
6. **alpine marmot**
7. **raven**
8. **alpine ibex**
9. **chamois**
10. **mountain chaffinch**
11. **weasel**
12. **small apollo butterfly**
13. **fieldmouse**

IN THE ALPS

For centuries, people in the Alps hunted the wild animals living there for survival and for sport, and many species came close to extinction. Now there are very strict laws protecting both animal and plant life, and hunting and fishing are carefully controlled. This policy has led to a gradual increase in the populations of most species, and it has allowed certain other animals to return—often for the first time in decades or even centuries—to regions from which they had been chased away by humans.

The wallcreeper has a gray body and red and black wings. A skillful climber, it rapidly scales vertical rock faces, poking its beak into cracks in search of the small insects on which it feeds.

Many species of flower have adapted successfully to the high mountain climate. This is a yellow gentian.

The chamois is an extremely nimble animal. It has short horns that curve back sharply.

Vipers do not lay eggs on the ground like other snakes. Instead, the eggs are kept inside the mother, and she gives birth to live young. The viper will not attack if it is left undisturbed.

Black grouse – During the mating season, the male black grouse hold "tournaments" in which they fight each other in specially marked patches of ground which are called arenas.

The alpine marmot is a large rodent that digs underground burrows. It is related to the squirrel.

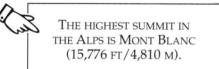

The golden eagle inhabits the highest and most inaccessible regions of the Alps. It is a solitary bird of prey which lives in pairs only for the purposes of incubating their eggs and raising their chicks. The golden eagle controls its territory by gliding around on currents of air, hunting both for its prey and for other birds of prey, which it aggressively chases away.

THE HIGHEST SUMMIT IN THE ALPS IS MONT BLANC (15,776 FT / 4,810 M).

HOOVES AND HORNS

The unique head ornaments and feet of many mountain animals, known as ungulates (hoofed animals), are their key to survival. Horns are powerful weapons used by ungulates for defense against predators and as a means to impose their authority on the herd. Hooves, which look as if they might easily slip, are in fact ideal for life on steep, rocky, and often snow-covered terrain. They allow the animals to climb and run with amazing speed and agility. The natural enemies of ungulates are birds of prey, such as the eagle, as well as bears, wolves, and lynx, which have begun to reappear in the Alps for the first time in centuries.

An alpine ibex pictured with its young.

When the chamois sets its foot on the ground, the toes split apart to give the animal a good grip, whether or not the ground is snow-covered.

The chamois generally lives above the tree line, but in winter heads down to lower elevations to live in the thick woods. Chamois live in small herds. The female gives birth to one kid, which is able to follow her just a few hours after being born.

The eagle often hunts for young ungulates, which it is able to snatch up in flight and carry away to its nest.

The alpine ibex is a massive ungulate with a short beard and large horns, which in the male can grow up to 3 ft (1 m) long.

The Alps are home to the wild rhododendron.

The mouflon is the only wild sheep living in Europe. The male has distinctive horns, which are wide at the base and curl to a sharp point around its ears. These horns grow throughout the animal's entire life.

Food – The mouflon is a herbivore and will often nibble on the bark of tender trees. If too much of the bark is gnawed away, the tree will die, since the sap that runs inside is no longer able to reach the leaves.

MARMOT

The tail of the marmot is short and covered with bristly fur, and its legs are short and stocky.

Found in many parts of the world, the marmot is a large rodent whose weight varies from 9 to 18 lb (4 to 8 kg), depending on the season. Like all rodents, it has very well-developed incisor teeth, which go on growing throughout its life. Young marmots have white incisors, while those of adults are a yellowish color. Humans have known about the marmot since ancient times. The Roman naturalist Pliny the Elder (23-79 A.D.) gave it the name Alpine Mouse and wrote that it "lived underground and whistled like a mouse." In winter, the marmot hibernates in its burrow, after stocking it with food to be eaten during its short waking periods. It does not reappear until the spring.

Behavior – Marmots spend a great deal of time around their burrows, seated on their hind legs, intently watching the surrounding area. Whenever they sense danger, they warn other marmots with a characteristic whistling sound.

Enemies – Among the marmot's enemies is the raven—a skillful predator that steals the marmot's young.

Other enemies

Ravens usually attack in large numbers, but the eagle arrives silently and alone. After spotting its prey from the air, the eagle dives down. As it approaches, it slows its fall, extends its legs, and opens its talons, snatching up its helpless victim. Eagles also hunt small ungulates, rabbits, hares, and snakes.

Marmots feed on roots, leaves, and grass. They eat sitting on their hind paws, holding their food between their front paws.

Fat – Beneath its fur, the marmot has a thick layer of fat that offers protection against the cold and also provides an extra supply of energy. Some people living in the Alps believe that the fat of a marmot helps cure respiratory illnesses.

Whistling – The marmot's whistle is not used just to warn of approaching danger. It is also a way for marmots to keep in contact with one another. Whenever they hear a warning whistle, all the marmots immediately rush back to their burrows, without waiting to determine the source of the danger. It seems that even chamois recognize the marmot's whistle as a signal that danger is near.

SAINT BERNARD

This large dog, with it's very thick black, white, and tan coat, was bred as early as the 18th century by monks living around the Great Saint Bernard hospice in the Swiss Alps. The Saint Bernard was bred for its sense of smell, which it uses to hunt for people buried in the snow by avalanches and landslides. The dogs are trained to dig down into the snow and drag people to safety.

Saint Bernards often wore a small barrel of brandy around their necks, to help relieve the people they rescued.

Heavy – Among the largest of all dogs, the Saint Bernard can weigh up to 176 lb (80 kg), but has a sweet, gentle temperament.

Edelweiss An extremely rare flower, the edelweiss is a protected species.

"Barry" was the most famous of all Saint Bernards. He lived from 1800 to 1814 and saved the lives of 40 people.

Temperate Forests

TEMPERATE FORESTS

The geographical zone that includes temperate forests extends from the edge of the tundra to subtropical regions. The vegetation includes coniferous trees, such as pine, larch, and fir, as well as deciduous trees like beech, oak, and birch. The undergrowth of shrubs and bushes in these forests is often thick and impenetrable. As a result, the snow often does not reach the ground and the animals are able to find some food. In winter, many other animals hibernate or migrate to warmer climates where food is more plentiful.

The porcupine is a nocturnal animal, whose body is covered with spines.

The squirrel is a small rodent that usually lives in trees, scurrying quickly up and down the branches.

Packs of wolves are always led by the strongest male.

Opossum – Common throughout North America and Australia, the opossum is a marsupial that, like the kangaroo, carries its young in a pouch on its stomach. When the young grow bigger, they are carried on their mother's back.

Brown bears – Adult bears are very heavy and usually find it hard to climb trees, but bear cubs love to climb. Mother bears are very protective of their cubs and will attack humans if they think their cubs are in danger.

The Japanese macaque is the only monkey that lives in a snowy region. Researchers have discovered that these animals have a complex way of communicating, which includes distinctive calls, shouts, and muttering sounds, as well as certain postures and gestures.

The lynx has been known to attack large animals, such as reindeer.

Skillful swimmer – The otter never strays far from the water. Its favorite food is fish, which it is able to hunt underwater.

European deer herds are composed of an adult male, together with a number of females (the harem) and their young. As long as the male retains its strength, none will dare to challenge his dominance over the harem.

Dam builders – Beavers cut branches and logs and weave them together skillfully with mud to make dams, which raise the level of the water in which they live. This ensures that their lodges, which are constructed inside the pond area formed by the dams, are well away from their predators.

WINTER IN THE FOREST

Hare – Leverets (young hares) find plenty of tender shoots and grasses to eat in the spring, but during the winter, when the few plants left over from the summer are covered with snow, they take refuge in their burrows.

During the winter, many plants die and others almost stop growing because of the cold. When food starts to grow scarce for herbivores, some will migrate toward southern regions where the climate is warmer. Others will climb into their underground burrows for a long sleep, called hibernation, which lasts throughout the winter months, and may include a few short waking periods. Their burrows are either dug into the earth or made in natural hollows, such as holes in tree trunks or caves. These burrows are often filled with food supplies gathered during the summer, even though the fat accumulated over the summer months may be all the animal needs for survival. Other animals neither hibernate nor migrate, but eat the sparse vegetation found in wooded areas not covered with snow.

Many hibernating animals stock their burrows with acorns and other types of food.

Hidden life – In winter, the woods seem to be deserted. In fact, they are always full of life. Mammals, reptiles, amphibians, and even insects take refuge in their burrows, spending the winter in hibernation as they wait for nature to reawaken in the spring.

The dormouse will often hide in the roofs of houses to keep warm.

Badgers spend the winter in underground burrows. Their young either remain with their mother or dig their own burrow.

Snowshoe hare – This animal's curious name comes from its large, furry back feet, which allow it to move around easily on the snow without sinking in.

Grizzly bear – The mother grizzly bear must feed her cubs large quantities of food during spring and summer so that they have enough energy for winter hibernation.

THE FORESTS OF CANADA

Great forests – Canada is a vast country, which stretches from coast to coast across the upper half of North America. Large portions of it are covered with dense forests. As one heads north, the forests of broad-leaved trees tend to make way for coniferous forests, which are more resistant to severe winter weather.

Animal life – These regions are home to many carnivores, including the common red and silver fox, the wolf, the wolverine, and the black bear—the latter prefers to feed on fruit, but will also feed on rodents.

1. crow
2. golden eagle
3. mountain goat
4. wapiti, or American elk
5. grizzly bear
6. black bear
7. white sheep
8. moose
9. wolverine
10. wolf
11. porcupine
12. lynx
13. salmon
14. otter
15. beaver
16. raccoon
17. cougar (or mountain lion)
18. pika, or 'calling hare'
19. hoary marmot

LYNX

Deer are the favorite prey of the lynx, but it will also attack domestic animals, such as sheep and goats.

The tail of the lynx is much shorter than those of other members of the cat family. While a long tail acts as a rudder, helping the animal to change directions quickly during a rapid chase, the lynx's short tail helps it to chase its prey over longer distances. The lynx's upper leg muscles are particularly well developed, enabling it to pounce from far away. Its natural habitats are woods and forests, where it lies in ambush among the branches.

The bobcat also lives in North America and is a close relative of the lynx. It prowls around by night, often close to villages and houses. Perfectly camouflaged among the trees, it is quite prepared to attack domestic animals. Its footprints in the snow, similar to those of a large domestic cat, provide the only clue to its presence.

Cubs – The female usually gives birth to two to four cubs in a den that she prepares in a well-hidden place, such as the hollow of a tree or a cave. The cubs remain with their mother until they are about ten months old, and then they leave the family. The lynx is a solitary animal, and maintains its own personal hunting territory.

The lynx has very strong, muscular back legs, which it uses to pounce on birds trying to fly away.

THE FORESTS OF AMERICA

The majestic deciduous forests of North America are vast areas of intact woodlands where animals live undisturbed. There are many lakes, rivers, and streams that help to sustain the large number of herbivores and carnivores.

Colors of the landscape – The colors of the animals match those of their forest habitat, helping them to stay hidden among the shadows and trees. This phenomenon is known as camouflage—a process of evolution and adaptation that makes it possible for animals—prey and predator alike—to improve their chances of survival.

1. Virginia opossum
2. flying squirrel
3. hairy woodpecker
4. northern flicker
5. cardinal
6. American gray fox
7. white-tailed deer
8. box turtle
9. skunk
10. white-footed mouse
11. wild turkey
12. cottontail

FORESTS OF THE UNITED STATES

The United States is a very large country with many different kinds of forest, both broad-leaf and coniferous. Because there are no mountain ranges running east to west, many animal species survived the ice age, when this region was covered with ice. Unlike many species in Europe and Asia, they were able to head toward warmer, southern climates without meeting any natural obstacles.

The cottontail rabbit hides during the day. At night it searches for grass, shoots, and bark to eat.

Opossum – Once the young become too large to travel in their mother's pouch, they are carried on her back.

A deer's antlers reveal its age only for the first few years of its life. It then becomes impossible to determine the animal's age accurately from its antlers.

The weasel is a very active carnivore that is capable of killing prey much larger than itself.

Californian redwood trees can reach heights of around 394 ft (120 m).

The skunk has a very unusual defensive weapon—it sprays a potent, foul-smelling odor at its predators from glands located under its tail. If the attacker persists, the skunk will make sure the animal stays away by spraying the liquid into its face.

SQUIRRELS

North America is home to several species of squirrel, a small, extremely agile rodent that spends much of its time in the trees, running up and down the topmost branches or leaping long distances from one branch to the next. Squirrels can be gray, black, or red, and can have long or short tails, and are of various sizes.

Diet – Squirrels love to eat seeds and nuts. With its strong front teeth, it has no trouble biting into the shells of pine cones, acorns, hickory nuts, and walnuts.

This squirrel skull illustrates the strength of the animal's front teeth.

Tail – Most squirrels have a long tail, which is covered with thick, bushy fur that helps the squirrel maintain its balance while it performs its characteristic acrobatic leaps.

Tamiasciurus is the scientific name of the American red squirrel, which is very similar to its European cousin, but is slightly larger.

DEER

The female deer is smaller than the male, and has no antlers. Deer have a reddish color in the summer, but this darkens during the winter months. The rear part of their bodies is pale in color. There are many sub-species of deer, such as the North American elk, or wapiti, which usually lives in forested areas, but which is also found in marshy regions where trees are scarce. If they are not disturbed too much, deer can adapt well to the presence of humans.

The fur of young deer is covered with characteristic light spots.

An adult male stands guard over its family while, in the background, two young males lock antlers in combat.

Antlers are bony outgrowths that grow rapidly, and are initially covered by a layer of fur known as 'velvet.' This layer quickly tears and falls away, leaving the antlers exposed. The deer helps the velvet come off by rubbing its antlers against tree trunks.

These four illustrations show how the antlers of a deer develop over a four-year period.

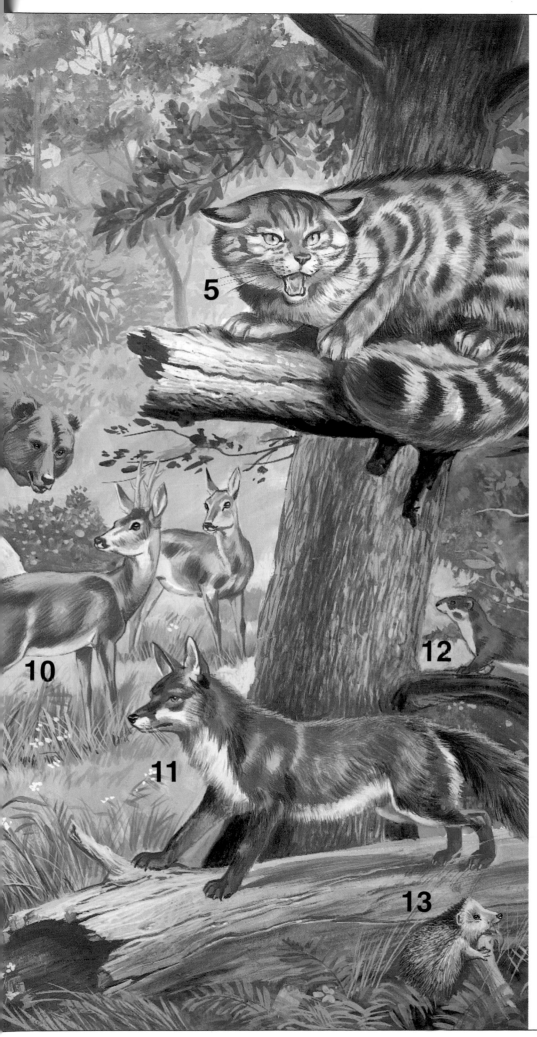

THE FORESTS OF EUROPE

Temperate climate – Europe lies between subtropical and arctic zones. It has a temperate climate, which means that although the winters are cold and the summers hot, the temperatures are never very extreme. Vegetation is mixed, and includes both evergreen and deciduous trees.

Fauna – Whereas in central and southern Europe the forests have been replaced over the centuries by farmland, in northern regions the forests have remained more or less intact. In spite of these differences, the fauna is largely similar all over Europe, and varies only according to the latitude of its habitats. In northern regions, where the winters are severe and the food scarce, the animals are mostly migratory species. In southern regions, most of the animals do not migrate.

1. red deer
2. squirrel
3. fallow deer
4. brown bear
5. wild cat
6. European boar
7. hare
8. European badger
9. polecat
10. roe deer
11. red fox
12. weasel
13. hedgehog
14. carrion crow
15. buzzard

EUROPEAN FORESTS

Unlike hares, wild rabbits dig deep burrows in the earth.

Except for the north-eastern regions, the number and size of forests in the European plains have decreased considerably in the last two centuries, although there are still some smaller forested areas in western and central regions. Mountain regions, however, are thickly forested, and so provide a vital sanctuary for many animal species. These species are increasingly protected by laws in the various countries where they are found.

The genet is a carnivore that looks very much like a cat. The only European country in which it is found is Spain.

Roe deer – The number of roe deer in Europe is growing fast. The male is a fierce defender of its territory. The female hides her calves among the vegetation while they are still young enough to be suckled. After three months, she takes them out into the open.

The dormouse is extremely common in wooded areas. Its reputation as a great sleeper perhaps comes from the fact that it hunts by night and sleeps during the day. It also hibernates in the winter.

These two examples of mushrooms are known as an amanita. The one with the white spots (*Amanita muscaria*) is poisonous, while the other (*Amanita caesarea*) is excellent for cooking. Never eat wild mushrooms without expert supervision.

The forest dormouse is a tiny rodent that eats almost anything, from grubs and insects to seeds, acorns, and chestnuts.

Despite its harmless appearance, the weasel is quite capable of killing all the chickens in a hen house, if it finds its way in.

The wild cat looks much like a domestic cat. Although it is often difficult to tell the two animals apart, the wild cat is slightly larger, heavier, and more agile. It feeds on squirrels, mice, small birds, and wildfowl, such as ducks and geese.

The marten is a member of the mustelid family, and preys on dormice, birds, and other animals, chasing them through the trees with great agility and often leaping acrobatically from one branch to another.

The stone marten is another mustelid which, unlike the marten, prefers to live on the ground. A carnivore, it often tries to break into hen houses at night.

The brown bear is a large, very shy animal that is rarely seen. It lives in the forest, eating its favorite foods—fruit and berries.

Bilberries, strawberries, raspberries, and huckleberries are among the brown bear's favorite foods.

The fox's reputation for great cunning probably derives from its mistrust of humans, who have hunted it relentlessly for centuries.

The hedgehog is covered with spines, which protect it against predators.

WILD BOAR

Acorns are the favorite food of the wild boar.

A relative of the domesticated pig, the wild boar lives in areas of thick undergrowth. Its coat is long and dark in the winter, but becomes shorter and lighter in the summer. Because it adapts very easily and eats a wide variety of food, including both plants and animals, it has a wide range and is found throughout Europe and Asia. The mother gives birth to between three and twelve very small young. After a few months, a number of mothers join together to form a herd.

Young boars – The mother never strays far from her young, because they are totally defenseless. Only when she is about to produce another litter will the mother push her young away from her, so that they can venture out into the world alone.

The bearded pig can weigh as much as 330 lb (150 kg). It has slender legs and a line of white fur stretching from its mouth to its ears. It lives in Southeast Asia.

The pygmy hog is much smaller than the European boar, and weighs only about 22 lb (10 kg). It is found only in Assam, in north-east India.

HEDGEHOG

This small animal has a very narrow snout and is commonly found in wooded areas, where it can hide from its enemies in the undergrowth. Its body is covered with short spines, which are really just modified hairs. The spines are found all over the hedgehog's body, except on its snout, head, and stomach. When raised, the hedgehog's sharp spines are a useful defensive weapon against attacking animals. The hedgehog is mainly an insectivore, but it will also feed on fruits, berries, acorns, and mushrooms.

There are usually five hedgehogs in a litter.

These tracks are those of a hedgehog that has awoken from hibernation and left its burrow to go hunting for food, leaving its footprints in the last snows of winter. Tracks such as these help us to understand animals' behavior and habits.

Rolled up – Hedgehogs are able to roll themselves up into a ball to protect the softer parts of their bodies, which have no spines.

Venom resistant
Hedgehogs are generally unaffected by snakes' poison, and they will attack and kill even vipers, which cannot easily bite through the hedgehog's spines.

Nocturnal hunter

After sunset, the hedgehog comes out of its burrow to hunt for snails, insects, millipedes, and other tiny creatures. It can also eat bees, hornets, and scorpions without worrying about being stung. It is very thorough in its search, turning over every leaf and twig. The mother takes her young along with her in order to teach them how to find food.

Hedgehogs eat plants such as mushrooms, fruit, berries, and lettuce.

The young – The mother hedgehog prepares quite a large, ground-level nest, which she builds out of leaves in an out-of-the-way place. On the day after her young are born, the mother hedgehog goes back to her search for food to ensure that her milk supply is good.

The porcupine is much larger than the hedgehog and, unlike the hedgehog, is a vegetarian rodent. There is a popular belief that the porcupine can throw its spines at aggressors, but this is untrue.

Fox

This nocturnal carnivore is a member of the canine, or dog, family, and has been the subject of countless fables and stories since ancient times. Foxes usually live alone, and they group together only to defend their territory.

All foxes have thick fur, but the length of their fur depends on the climate.

Tail – The white tip of the mother fox's thick tail helps her cubs to find their way in the darkness of the forest.

Litter – A fox's litter usually contains four to six cubs, but rarely do more than three cubs survive the first few days of life. This ensures that only the strongest grow into adults and reproduce.

CAVES

The fate of the bat is a very sad one. Because people find bats ugly, and believe that they are dirty and dangerous, they have hunted them mercilessly. In reality, however, bats are quite harmless, and are fearful of humans. They are also very useful, because they feed on insect pests, some of which are harmful to crops. The bat begins its hunt for food at sunset and, like the swallow, catches insects in flight.

Some bats feed on fruit or nectar.

As it flies, the bat emits high-pitched sounds, which humans can't hear. These sounds bounce back off the insect, allowing the bat to locate its prey.

Living in the darkness – By day, bats sleep in caves, along with a number of other animals that do not need light in their daily lives. Some bats are even blind and some, like the olm salamander, have eyes that have gradually fallen into disuse.

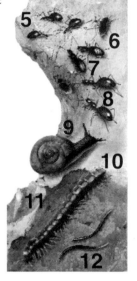

1. western pipistrel
2. long-eared bat
3. eyeless amphipod
4. olm
5. blind beetle
6. bathysciola beetle
7. speomolopo
8. blind rhadinid beetle
9. subtroglofilo
10. brown centipede
11. cave shrimp
12. millipede

HARE AND WILD RABBIT

The legs of the hare are longer than those of the rabbit, allowing it to move faster.

These two rodents look very much alike, but actually there are major differences between them. Rabbits are smaller than hares, and their legs and ears are shorter. They dig underground burrows, while hares only dig shallow depressions in the ground. Humans have introduced wild rabbits to regions where they are not native and have few enemies, such as Australia, Chile, and New Zealand. The resulting overpopulation of rabbits has had a disastrous effect on crops.

The hare, unlike the wild rabbit, has a highly developed sense of territory. During the mating season, males compete for females by dueling with their front legs, like boxers.

Litters – Mother rabbits dig burrows up to 6.5 ft (2 m) deep, with several exits. They generally give birth to five or six young at a time. After only three weeks, the young rabbits are ready to go out and explore the world.

The rabbit's survival usually depends on its ability to escape quickly.

The first days of life – Young hares, unlike young rabbits, are born with fur, and are active and able to see.

BROWN BEAR

Up until about five hundred years ago, the brown bear was common throughout Europe and central and northern Asia. Sadly, it was ruthlessly hunted by humans over the centuries, and now survives in only a few mountain areas, situated far apart from each other. Nowadays, the spread of knowledge about nature and wildlife has calmed many old fears and myths surrounding this peaceful animal, and European countries have imposed strict laws protecting the bear. Bears are rarely seen in the wild because they avoid humans, but they can be found in the Pyrenees, the Alps, Scandinavia, and Russia.

Bears are particularly fond of honey, although this is not a regular part of their diet.

Adaptability – Only an animal such as the bear, which is capable of surviving in a range of very different environments, can have such a varied habitat. Bears live in the coniferous forests of the north, as well as in the deciduous forests of the south.

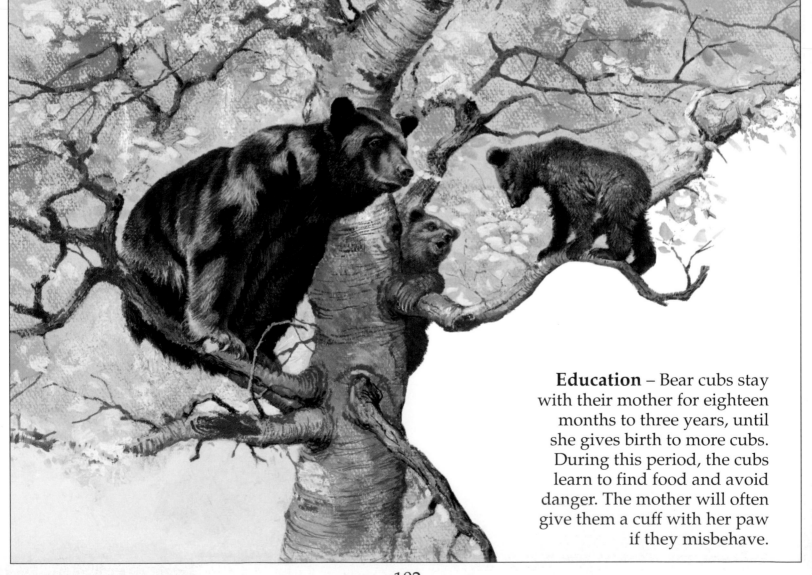

Education – Bear cubs stay with their mother for eighteen months to three years, until she gives birth to more cubs. During this period, the cubs learn to find food and avoid danger. The mother will often give them a cuff with her paw if they misbehave.

Greedy for honey – Bears love to raid beehives, which they find in the holes of tree trunks, and eat the sweet honey. Their thick fur generally protects them from beestings, however, too many stings on the nose and tongue may force them to retreat!

Food – Bears are omnivores, meaning they feed on plants, such as fruits, berries, shoots, mushrooms, and roots, but they will also eat meat and fish, whenever they can find it. In areas where they still roam wild, bears often do not fear humans, and will sometimes rampage through campsites in search of food. That is why park wardens warn tourists not to feed bears or leave food out unprotected.

Bears are very fond of berries, especially the blueberry and European bilberry.

103

BIRDS OF EUROPE

Temperate zones are perfect for birds, and bushes, trees, and rocks offer unlimited possibilities for building nests that are beyond the reach of predators. These regions also provide plenty of food, including both seeds and fruit, and animals such as insects, grubs, worms, and water creatures. During the day, forests and fields are filled with hundreds of different songs, which birds use both to mark their territories and to find nesting partners.

At night, nocturnal birds take the place of the diurnal birds (those that are active during the day), and the unmistakable melody of the nightingale and the monotonous "whoo-whoo" of the owl are to be heard. Birdwatching is a favorite hobby among nature lovers. Well hidden and armed with a strong pair of binoculars, birdwatchers delight in identifying and studying bird species in their natural habitat.

Woodpeckers are commonly found in forests where they flit swiftly from one tree to another. They use their beaks to make small holes in the bark, hunting for the grubs and insects that they love to eat.

Peregrine falcons sometimes even nest in the city.

The peregrine falcon is found on almost every continent. It is a very adaptable bird, and will nest on rocks, in trees, and on the ground. Fledglings (young birds) are able to fly at one month, but they continue to demand food from their parents.

Feeders set out during the winter months can attract many different birds.

A bird feeder can be made from an ordinary cardboard box.

1. black-bellied plover
2. long-tailed jaeger
3. turtledove
4. redstart
5. Manx shearwater
6. quail
7. alpine swift
8. swift
9. swallow
10. martin
11. golden plover
12. spoonbill
13. redwing
14. starling
15. lapwing
16. golden oriole
17. pintail
18. Canada goose
19. jack snipe

Ducks – A pair of mallards are shown here with their ducklings swimming along behind them. Just a few hours after they have hatched, the ducklings are able to follow their mother through the ponds and rivers that provide their food.

Many species – Temperate zones are home to an enormous variety of birds: from the swift, which spends much of its life in flight, to the plover, which toddles around on the ground in search of food, to the shearwater, which is found along the seacoasts and out at sea.

☞ THE TOP FLYING SPEED OF THE SWIFT: 125 MPH· (200 KM/H).

Unlike other vultures, which feed on dead meat, the bearded vulture eats only bones.

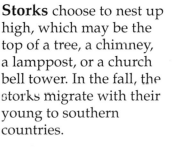

Storks choose to nest up high, which may be the top of a tree, a chimney, a lamppost, or a church bell tower. In the fall, the storks migrate with their young to southern countries.

MEADOWS

Many animals make their nests in the thick grasses of meadows. Insects, small reptiles, and mammals live among the blades of grass, while beneath the surface, the soil teems with insect larvae, worms, and moles. During the cold season, many of these little animals disappear, either because they go into hibernation or because they have come to the end of a part of their life cycle. In the second case, the animals' eggs and larvae lie ready to fill the meadow with life again as soon as spring returns.

The wasp's black and yellow coloring acts as a warning to predators. In fact, the wasp is feared by most animals and by people, because of its very painful, irritating sting.

The dandelion is found in meadows and gardens all over Europe and North America.

1. carabus beetle	9. blind-worm
2. toad	10. snail
3. goldsmith beetle	11. green toad
4. goldsmith beetle larva	12. wood mouse
5. mole cricket	13. wood mouse nest
6. mole cricket larva	14. mole
7. lizard	15. cricket
8. lizard eggs	16. earthworm

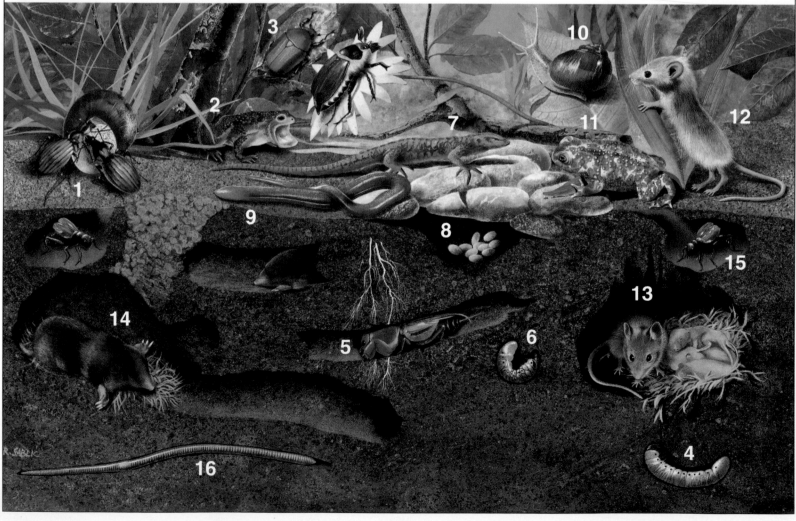

Delicate balance – Weed-killers (herbicides) are often used in meadows and gardens to destroy weeds that are out of control. Unfortunately, such products also kill countless numbers of insects, and this in turn leads to the disappearance of many other animals that normally depend on the insects as a source of food. The result is a tidy-looking meadow with few creatures living in it.

1. bumblebee	9. quail
2. cabbage butterfly	10. lark
3. sparrow	11. praying mantis
4. cabbageworm	12. tortoiseshell
5. red admiral	13. blue butterfly
6. swallowtail butterfly	14. snail
7. swallowtail caterpillar	15. grasshopper
8. green lizard	16. bee
	17. goldsmith beetle
	18. wasp

The harvest mouse is so tiny and light that it can climb up a wheat stalk almost without bending it.

One of the most charming and timid of meadow animals is the wild rabbit.

RIVERS

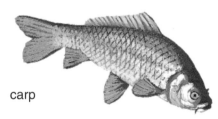

barbel

Along their route to the sea, rivers receive a constant supply of water from the ice and snow in the mountains, as well as from the rain collected in lakes and streams.

1. stickleback
2. trout
3. dace
4. whitefish
5. sturgeon
6. otter
7. eel
8. dory
9. pike

The tumbling and mixing of river water provides much of the oxygen that aquatic animals need to survive. Some of these animals, such as crayfish and trout, are especially vulnerable to pollution, and are the first to disappear if harmful substances, such as industrial or city waste, are poured into the river. Even the barbel, which feeds on small organisms living on the riverbed, needs clean water to survive.

carp

Carp prefer to live in still waters and move slowly along the muddy depths of the river, searching for food on the riverbed. Carp sometimes grow very large, but, luckily for them, people do not find them very tasty.

THE AMAZON RIVER IS THE BIGGEST RIVER IN THE WORLD, IF MEASURED BY THE AMOUNT OF WATER THAT FLOWS THROUGH IT.

Other river creatures – Fish and other aquatic animals are not the only species that make the river their home. Many other animals depend on the river as a source of food. These include the kingfisher, a bird which feeds on small fish, and the dragonfly, which, in its larval stage, lives in the water and feeds on water insects, small fish, and tadpoles.

When a trout sees a fly passing above the surface of the river, it will leap out of the water to catch it in flight.

109

MARSHLANDS

The favorite habitat of many water birds, marshlands provide an abundant source of food. Some birds, like the heron, have long legs and beaks, and feed on fish and frogs that live in the shallow water. Others, like ducks, have wide beaks, which they use to scoop up food they find floating on the surface.

Whether as a tadpole or as an adult, the frog is one of the favorite foods of many marsh birds.

A male mallard swoops down to land on the water.

Flying in formation – Ducks, geese, and a few other birds fly in formation to save energy. Those behind the lead bird are protected somewhat from air currents, and so they do not have to flap as hard. From time to time the lead bird falls back to rest, allowing another bird to take its place.

Grasslands and Savannah

PREDATOR AND PREY

Wherever the land is flat and vegetation scarce, there are few hiding places, and it is easy to see and be seen. Animals that live on the prairies, plains, and savannahs (areas that are rich in grass but poor in trees and bushes) have colors that help them blend into the environment, making them almost invisible. Only big animals, like elephants, which live in large herds and are well able to defend themselves, can afford not to worry about predators. These animals are able to graze in peace, keeping a close eye on their young, which are the only ones among them who may be threatened by predators.

The cheetah is an elegant member of the cat family with thickly spotted fur. Its slender, agile body, its small, light head, and its long, mobile tail are all perfectly suited to quick chases.

Impalas live in small groups, in grassy regions where the vegetation is not too thick. They need to stay close to water, because they must drink every day. In times of drought, when little or no rain falls, the impala migrates over long distances in search of water.

Lion – Although it is known as the "king of the jungle," the lion in fact prefers the open areas of the savannah. There, it is not easily seen because of its coat, which is the color of dried grass. The male lion has a long, thick mane.

A giraffe runs from a predator. The giraffe's ability to run fast is its most effective form of defense.

A quick chase – A cheetah pounces on its prey. Although it is very fast, the cheetah cannot keep running for long. If it does not catch its prey the first time, it will give up the hunt and rest before trying again. Once the cheetah has chosen its prey, it will try to catch only that animal, even if it sights others during the chase.

The cheetah is the only member of the cat family (feline) that does not have retractable claws as an adult.

The prairie dog is a large rodent of the North American plains. It spends much of its time sitting in an erect position, watching for danger. It gets its name from its characteristic call, which sounds like a dog's bark.

A mother coyote teaches her young to hunt for rabbits on the North American prairie.

The spotted-tail native cat, or quoll, is actually an Australian marsupial, and not a cat at all. It is a nocturnal carnivore, although it will also eat plants.

Cape hunting dogs are direct descendants of wolves, foxes, and jackals. Like wolves, they have developed an effective group hunting technique, which allows them to capture much larger animals, like zebras.

NORTH AMERICAN PRAIRIES

The Great Plains – In the vast open spaces of the Great Plains, where great herds of bison once roamed free, American settlers fenced off large areas of the countryside with barbed wire. Even so, today there are still large areas of uncultivated land where animals—from the bison to the rattlesnake—are now protected by law.

Where two worlds clashed – Native Americans depended on hunting animals of the prairie, especially the American bison, for their survival. But the first white settlers were farmers whose farmland and crops could be ruined by herds of bison and other prairie animals. They saw animals—the bison in particular—as a problem. To settle the West, and to deprive the free-roaming native peoples of their way of life, millions of bison were slaughtered. The conflict between the two different cultures over the land and the animals on it was long and bloody.

Large ungulates – Unlike the dry African savannah, where dozens of species of wild ungulates live, the North American prairie is home to only two characteristic species: the bison (commonly called the 'buffalo') and the pronghorn.

1. **American bison**
2. **coyote**
3. **pronghorn**
4. **prairie dog**
5. **rattlesnake**
6. **ground squirrel**
7. **sage grouse**
8. **horned lark**
9. **burrowing owl**

ON THE PRAIRIE

Terrible slaughters of animals were carried out by white settlers in the late eighteenth and nineteenth centuries. The American bison, in particular, was reduced from a population of some 60 million to just a few thousand. Among the most famous hunters was Colonel William Cody, better known as "Buffalo Bill." Because the bison is now protected, its numbers are increasing again.

The bobcat, or red lynx, lives in different regions throughout North America. A shy creature, it avoids contact with other animals and with humans. When chased by hunting dogs, it has been seen to climb to the top of a prickly cactus without suffering any ill effects.

A mother bison watches over her defenseless newborn calf.

Bison are large herbivores, which appear to be peaceful animals. They can in fact be very dangerous, especially when they believe that their young are in danger.

Prairie dogs live in very large colonies and dig networks of underground tunnels that are so extensive they are known as "townships." These rodents were also hunted and nearly exterminated in the early twentieth century.

The male sage grouse attracts a mate by displaying its colorful plumage. It will also defend its mating territory by engaging in fierce battles with other males.

COYOTE

This member of the dog, or canine, family has a highly developed ability to adapt to different surroundings. The coyote lives throughout North American, from the cold regions of Alaska to the tropics of Costa Rica. It has also successfully taken over the territory of wolves, which have been hunted almost to extinction. Because there are so many of them, humans generally try to control their population. Usually this does not work, because the coyote is a clever, careful animal. Coyotes live in small family groups.

Family – The coyote, unlike many other animals, will not go to great lengths to defend its hunting territory. But it is very protective of its family's territory, especially when its young are still small and unable to look after themselves.

Food – The coyote is a carnivore that prefers to hunt live prey, but which will also eat carrion, or animals killed by other predators. Its diet also includes various kinds of plants, such as fruits, berries, and some grasses.

NATIVE AMERICANS USED TO IMITATE THE CRY OF THE COYOTE AS A SIGNAL.

Because coyotes prey on many domestic animals, such as sheep and calves, they often clash with humans.

BISON

The bison is a large bovine (member of the ox family). Its body is unevenly proportioned, with the front part much bigger and more powerful than the back. Even its coat is not the same all over its body: its fur is long and thick at the front, but short around its hind legs. The male can weigh as much as a ton, while females are smaller. Their horns are not particularly long, and they fight by butting each other. Bison live in herds on the Great Plains, where there are not many trees. Generally, adult males make up one type of herd, which remains separate from those made up of females and calves.

During the winter, when the prairie is covered with snow, the bison digs into the snow with its hooves and muzzle to reach the grass on which it feeds.

Saved from extinction – In 1901, following the terrible bison slaughter of the 1800s, a group of committed naturalists founded the American Bison Society, which was dedicated to protecting this animal. A nature reserve for the protection of the bison was created, and this would later lead the governments of the United States and Canada to build similar nature reserves and parks for the conservation of wildlife.

Calves – The female bison gives birth to one calf each year.

European bison nearly became extinct during this century, but some still survive in zoos. They have been bred in captivity and a few have been reintroduced into the wild areas of Poland.

The European bison is taller and less heavily built than the American bison.

European bison

Skillful swimmer – Bison herds often move in search of new pastureland. During their migrations, they sometimes come across rivers, but these pose no problem for them, because they can swim without difficulty.

Defending their young – Like all animals, bison defend their families with all their might. Bison have been known to charge at tourists who get too close to their young.

GREAT PLAINS OF SOUTH AMERICA

From Venezuela to Tierra del Fuego – In addition to the Argentine plains, or pampas (which have little forest vegetation), there are similar great plains in Venezuela, known as *llanos*. There is also the great rain basin of the Amazon River, which is covered with a dense tropical forest, and where the animals are entirely different.

Argentina – This large South American country is almost entirely flat. Few people live outside the major cities and towns, especially in the Patagonia region in the south. The climate is hot in the north, but grows gradually colder toward the south. This explains the variety of animal species that live there.

1. **giant anteater**
2. **mara**
3. **rhea**
4. **pampas deer**
5. **giant armadillo**
6. **capybara**
7. **agouara or maned wolf**
8. **giant paca**
9. **golden agouti**
10. **viscacha**
11. **chaja or crested screamer**
12. **armadillo**
13. **wild rabbit**
14. **jaguarundi**

THE PAMPAS

Because of the low rainfall and scarce vegetation, the pampas cannot sustain large animal populations. This vast area is nonetheless home to a wide variety of animal species, which often come into contact with the many cattle herds that roam freely, watched over by the *gauchos*, or Argentinian cowboys. The pampas once covered a much larger area than they do today, but they have now been reduced to a number of small protected areas inside national parks. The remainder of the land previously occupied by the pampas is now used for agriculture or as pastureland for cattle.

The peccary is similar to the wild boar, but smaller. It lives in packs of around ten members, and is quick to attack when in danger.

An unusual mammal, the armadillo is covered with protective armor. Its diet is varied, and includes small animals and insects, as well as roots and berries. Its underground burrows are often quite deep.

The rhea is similar to the African ostrich, but smaller, and can grow to over 5 ft (1.7 m) tall. The male hatches the eggs, and will attack anything that approaches— including females trying to lay more eggs in the same nest!

The jaguarundi is the predator of the pampas. It has a long tail and dark coloring, and is a solitary creature that hunts mainly at night for small mammals.

The small, but sturdy Argentine horse is the inseparable working companion of the gaucho.

Perched on a tree branch, a red ovenbird watches as a crested screamer passes by. A bird of ancient origin, the screamer works through marshy regions in search of choice plants.

The pampas deer is smaller than the European deer, and it has a light coat that allows it to blend into its surroundings. The horns of its antlers have only three points.

The mara (also known as the Patagonian hare) is pictured here with its young, which remains with its mother for nine months. A skillful runner and jumper, the mara digs very deep burrows.

The giant anteater has an extremely long tongue that it uses to catch ants and termites. It feeds by digging into an anthill with its large front claws, and inserts its tongue into the tunnels. The insects then become stuck to the tongue.

THE TONGUE OF THE ANTEATER CAN BE AROUND 3 FEET (1 M) LONG.

123

OPEN SPACES

Savannah – This picture shows a typical African savannah region, with the famous extinct volcano Mount Kilimanjaro in the background. The savannah is a vast grassy plain with only the occasional tree, such as a leafy acacia or the majestic baobab. For most of the year, the grass is dry and yellowish in color. It turns green only after the rains fall, during a brief period in which the vegetation begins to grow again.

Many animal species live and feed in the savannah. Large herbivores that can be seen from far away find protection in big herds. Smaller animals hide from predators in the tall grass.

1. warthog
2. lesser kudu
3. oryx
4. African vulture
5. African elephant
6. giraffe
7. zebra
8. blue duiker
9. impala
10. vulturine guinea fowl
11. francolin
12. genet
13. lion

LION

Although it is known as the 'king of the jungle,' the lion actually lives mainly in the open savannah. Its other title, the 'king of the beasts,' probably refers to the dignified and aloof manner in which lions will choose resting spots in places where they are able to see for long distances all around. This wide view of its hunting grounds allows the lion to work out the best plan of attack to capture its prey without being seen. The lion appears to be a lazy animal, because it spends long periods dozing. Only when it is hungry or has to defend its territory, does it shake itself out of its torpor, or inactivity.

Adult lions are very patient with their cubs, and do not react to bites and scratches.

The lion's most famous feature is its thick mane, which is present only on the male and is found on no other member of the cat family.

Hunting is usually carried out by groups of females. The male rarely takes part. The hunting females surround their prey, crouching low in the tall grass. When the targeted animals sense the danger, they gallop away in panic. But this reaction generally leads them straight to other lionesses lying in wait.

Family – Lions hunt together in groups, unlike cheetahs and tigers, which hunt alone. In this way, family groups stay together for a long time, and grown cubs are not forced out on their own unless food becomes scarce in their hunting territory.

During the hottest part of the day, lions like to stretch out in the shade or play with their cubs.

Lion cubs – Lionesses give birth to an average of three cubs. During the two years it takes for them to become independent, their parents teach them everything they need to know to survive.

A hyena circles around a lioness that has killed a zebra. When the lions have finished eating, hyenas will eat the remains.

THE FANGS OF THE LION CAN GROW TO 3 IN (7 CM) LONG.

133

ELEPHANT

The African Elephant almost became extinct during the late nineteenth and early twentieth centuries. During this time it was hunted extensively for its ivory tusks. Also, humans made great changes to its natural habitat. Now elephants live mostly in large national parks, studied by zoologists and protected by game wardens. Sadly, this is still not enough to prevent their being killed in large numbers by poachers, who shoot the animals down undetected. Unlike the African elephant, the Asian elephant has never been in danger, because it has been used for centuries as a working animal.

Mealtime – Like the giraffe, the elephant sometimes likes to eat leaves, which it pulls off the tree with its trunk. To reach its food, it will sometimes knock down the whole tree.

Baby elephants are sometimes hunted by lions, although the mother elephant will often chase the predators away.

Tusks and trunk – An elephant's tusks and trunk are very important for its survival. It uses its tusks to defend itself from predators and to dig for water in the ground during times of drought. With its highly flexible trunk, it pulls leaves from the trees and also sucks in water, which it then sprays into its mouth. Elephants love water. They will immerse themselves in water whenever they get the chance, and they are also skillful swimmers.

In the shade – Elephants love to stand in the shade to stay cool, because they are so massive that they cannot disperse the heat from their bodies very well. They also keep cool by fanning their ears back and forth in a rhythmic motion.

Just like children holding their mother's hand, baby elephants allow themselves to be led around by grabbing hold of their mother's tail with their trunk.

AN AFRICAN ELEPHANT CAN WEIGH AS MUCH AS SIX TONS.

The thin layer of dust that covers the elephant's body stops it from being bitten by parasites.

Dust baths – After having a bath in the river, or taking a shower by spraying water on its back with its trunk, the elephant will often have a dust bath, which helps protect it from parasites. Some birds help elephants by standing on their backs and feeding on the parasites.

OSTRICH

The ostrich is a bird that has adapted to its environment in quite a few amazing ways. It is the world's largest bird and can weigh more than 287 lb (130 kg). With its long neck, the ostrich can grow up to 8 ft (2.5 m) tall. Their flexible heads and their keen eyesight allow ostriches to spy danger from high up over great distances. With their long legs, they can reach speeds of up to 43 mph (70 km/h), which is usually more than fast enough to keep them safe from predators. Although the ostrich has long body and tail feathers, it cannot fly. The feathers were inherited from the ostrich's ancestors, which were able to fly.

Habitat – Ostriches prefer to live in open spaces, where they can see a long way and where they can run without meeting obstacles. They live on plants and small animals.

The mother ostrich abandons her young when they are just a few months old.

Living in groups – Ostriches do not live alone, but in groups of various sizes. While they search for food, at least one bird will act as a guard, watching the horizon closely for enemies, usually cheetahs and lions.

Ostriches have long eyelashes, which protect their eyes from the strong African sun and from the dust blown around by the wind.

Ostrich nests are made in depressions, hollowed out in the sandy soil and covered with soft material. Females hatch the eggs by day, and their gray coloring provides perfect camouflage. Males, whose coloring is mostly black, hatch the eggs by night.

Female ostriches lay between three and eight eggs each in a shared nest, and take turns to hatch them. The eggs each weigh over 3.3 lb (1.5 kg) and have very tough shells.

The beak of an ostrich is short, flat, and very strong. It is not adapted for eating any particular kind of food, but is used to chew grass and other plants, as well as to catch insects, small mammals, and snakes.

An ostrich chick can take a whole day to break the shell of its egg and struggle out. The first picture shows the difference in size between an ostrich egg and a hen's egg

RHINOCEROS

Despite its great size, the African rhinoceros is very skillful in the chase, and can change directions amazingly quickly.

The rhinoceros is found in Africa and Asia. It is one of the bigger members of the pachyderm family, which includes other thick-skinned animals like the elephant and the hippopotamus. In Africa, there are two rhinoceros species that are different from those found in Asia. They have two horns, and they have gradually adapted to their surrounding environment, with its open spaces and lack of tall vegetation. The Asian rhinoceros has only one horn and prefers to live in the thick of the forest.

The rhinoceros is at risk of extinction, because poachers hunt it ruthlessly for its horns, which are considered very valuable in some countries.

Peaceful grazing – Grazing rhinoceroses are always accompanied by cattle egrets, which feed on the insects disturbed by the animals' legs. Oxpeckers, on the other hand, ride on the rhinoceros's back to feed on the parasites in its skin. The rhinoceros loves water. It will often take long baths and, like the elephant, also likes to roll around in the mud, or in the dust, to rid itself of parasites and to keep cool.

Young rhinoceroses – A female rhinoceros usually gives birth to one young, every two or four years. The mother stays with her calf for a long time, even when the calf is quite well grown and independent.

THE HORN OF THE
WHITE RHINOCEROS CAN
BE AS MUCH AS 5 FT
(1.5 M) LONG.

Battles – Male rhinoceroses, like males of many other species, battle with each other to determine who will be the leading animal. Although they do use their horns, they use the side of the horn, rather than the point, as if they were fighting each other with sticks. Sometimes the horn will break off during such fights, but it will grow back again, though very slowly.

Sight and smell – The rhinoceros has very poor eyesight, and can see things only from close up, rather like a short-sighted human. Nevertheless, its sense of smell, like its hearing, is excellent and it can detect the presence of food or enemies from far away.

Growing up – The newborn rhinoceros can follow its mother around after just one hour, and usually either walks in front of her or at her side. The calf suckles for a year, and during this time it will grow from 110 lb (50 kg) to around 660 lb (300 kg).

The head of the rhinoceros is like that of many prehistoric animals.

THE FORESTS OF AUSTRALIA

Few people – Australia is still quite sparsely populated, because it was not colonized until relatively recently. Human settlements are found mostly along the coasts, especially on the eastern side. The central regions of the country are made up of vast areas of barren land.

Strange animals – The animals of Oceania, the continent that includes Australia, are very unusual and are not found on any other continent. Humans have introduced some new animals, such as the rabbit, which has caused a great deal of damage to agriculture, because of the rate at which its numbers increased.

1. and 2. sugar glider
3. rainbow lorikeet
4. cuscus
5. Tasmanian wolf (now extinct)
6. wallaby
7. emu
8. kangaroo
9. koala
10. monitor lizard
11. spiny anteater
12. duck-billed platypus

THE ANIMALS OF AUSTRALIA

Most Australian mammals are marsupials, which means that they have pouches on their stomachs. Their young are very tiny when they are born, and are unable to do virtually anything. Immediately after their birth, they make their way into the mother's stomach pouch. Her milk flows through the wall of the pouch, and the young animal laps up the milk with its tongue, gradually growing stronger.

In the nineteenth century, settlers introduced the rabbit, which rapidly increased in number, causing great damage to the crops. In an effort to stop the plague of rabbits from spreading further, the red fox was introduced. The fox has caused the extinction of other animals.

Emu – At around 6.5 ft (2 m) high, the emu is Australia's ostrich. It lives in large herds, which are always on the move, searching for areas with water. The female lays large green eggs, which are hatched by the male.

Australia – Australia is the largest island in Oceania, which is sometimes called the Fifth Continent. There are not very many species of animal living there, and there are no native monkeys, pachyderms, or ruminants. Many animals have since been introduced to the country by settlers.

The cockatoo is a big parrot, which is pure white in color. It has a long plume of yellow feathers sticking out from the back of its head, but nobody knows quite why it is there.

The honey possum is a tiny nocturnal marsupial, which travels from flower to flower, sucking in the nectar with its long, thin tongue, rather like a butterfly or a hummingbird. This is very unusual behavior for a mammal.

The common opossum is another nocturnal marsupial that lives among the trees. It has a prehensile tail, which means that it can hang on to tree branches by its tail, just like a monkey. It feeds on leaves and bark, but will also eat other animals' eggs. Opossums do not run away from humans, and often they will even form large, noisy colonies near houses.

With its striped coat and its long, bushy tail, the small numbat is unmistakable. It uses its long, thin tongue to explore holes in wood in search of the termites it loves to eat.

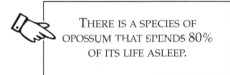

THERE IS A SPECIES OF OPOSSUM THAT SPENDS 80% OF ITS LIFE ASLEEP.

Although the spiny anteater looks like a hedgehog, it is in fact a very different creature. Like other marsupials, their young develop in a pouch, sucking on milk that flows through the mother's skin. Because of the sharp spines that cover their bodies, they have practically no natural enemies, except for the aboriginal, or native, people, who sometimes kill them for food.

MARSUPIALS

Marsupials are typically Australian mammals, although they are also found in both American continents. The opossum, for example, can be widely found in North America.

When they are born, young marsupials are still tiny embryos, no more than 0.4 to 0.8 in (1 to 2 cm) long, totally blind, and hairless. Development then continues in the mother's pouch, where the newborn remains for a period of weeks or months. When it finally emerges from the pouch, it is as if it were being born a second time.

The wombat lives in Australia's southern regions, digging deep burrows, which are composed of many interconnecting tunnels. It eats roots, leaves, and mushrooms.

The numbat is not much larger than a rat.

Kangaroo – Perhaps the best-known of all marsupials, the kangaroo moves very quickly by making great jumps, using only its back legs. A vegetarian, it eats grass, leaves, and the bark of trees.

The sugar glider looks rather like a squirrel and, like the squirrel, also lives in the trees. Its legs are joined by a membrane of skin, which acts as a parachute and allows the animal to glide through the air from tree to tree.

The spotted cuscus lives in the trees, and carries its young on its back until they are able to live on their own.

The extinct Tasmanian wolf looked like a dog. It was very aggressive and hunted at night.

The Tasmanian wolf was among the few meat-eating marsupials. Little is known about its habits, because it became extinct in 1933 in Tasmania, the only area in which it was found, and where it was likely ruthlessly hunted by humans.

THE SMALLEST OF ALL MARSUPIALS IS THE LITTLE PLANIGALE, WHICH IS ONLY 1.8 IN (4.5 CM) LONG.

Although Lumholtz's tree kangaroo lives in the trees, feeding on leaves, it is not considered a very skillful climber.

Tasmanian devil – This creature is found only in Tasmania. A carnivore, it hides in the thick of the forest by day and comes out at night. It is very aggressive, and can even defeat a dog in a fight. And yet, if it is reared with people from infancy, it can be easily tamed, and is affectionate toward humans.

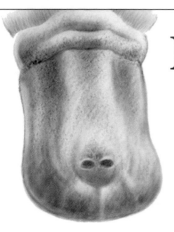

DUCK-BILLED PLATYPUS

The duck-billed platypus is a primitive animal with some very unique features. It has a wide, spatula-shaped bill, much like a duck's in appearance. Although it is a mammal, it lays eggs, usually two at a time. The eggs have a soft, rubbery shell, and the mother hatches them in the nest for about ten days. The young are born blind and hairless, and the mother suckles them while lying on her back. The young suck the milk as it seeps through her fur. When they are big enough, the mother takes them out with her to catch tiny underwater creatures.

The platypus's body is well suited to life in the water. On land, however, the platypus is clumsy and finds it hard to move around.

Bill – A platypus's bill is not really much like a bird's beak. Wide and flat, it has no teeth, but it does have two horny plates. The platypus does in fact have two teeth, which are on its tongue. It uses these teeth to grind its food, crushing it against the upper surface of its bill, which has a series of horny ridges.

The entrance to the platypus's burrow is dug directly into the banks of the rivers and streams in which it lives.

Habitat – The platypus spends much of its life in burrows that it digs close to the streams and rivers in which it lives. Early in the morning and late in the evening, it leaves its burrow to hunt for small aquatic animals such as grubs, worms, small fish, and crustaceans. It moves easily in water, thanks to its streamlined body and its webbed feet, which are perfect for swimming.

KOALA

The koala is a marsupial that looks like a teddy bear and weighs up to 33 lb (15 kg). It has gray fur, which is lighter around its stomach. Because its front paws have very strong claws, the koala is a strong and skillful climber, and is well-suited to its life among the trees. It spends much of its time in trees and rarely comes down to the ground. Koalas live in eastern Australia, where the forests are especially rich in eucalyptus trees.

The koala eats about 2.2 lb (1 kg) of eucalyptus leaves every day.

Diet – Koalas eat only eucalyptus leaves, and prefer old leaves to new, tender leaves. Zoologists have discovered that koalas do not eat new eucalyptus leaves because they contain a powerful poison called prussic acid.

Agile – Although koalas look quite stout and heavy, they are in fact very agile animals, and can jump easily from one branch to another and from one tree to another. They come down to the ground only when the trees are too far apart, and they usually spend their whole time among the branches of eucalyptus trees.

After a young koala becomes too big for its mother's pouch, it is carried on her back.

THE KOALA DOES NOT SUFFER FROM PARASITES, BECAUSE ITS FUR SMELLS OF EUCALYPTUS.

THE BIRDS OF OCEANIA

Emu chicks take two months to hatch out of their eggs. When they are born, they are covered with striped down.

Oceania is home to many spectacular bird species, such as the lyre bird and the bird of paradise. Perhaps surprisingly, the beauty of their feathers is rarely matched by a beautiful song. There are many species of parrot in Oceania, such as cockatoos, with their variety of colorful crests. Their plumage also varies, from the black feathers of the black cockatoo, to the white coloring of the sulfur-crested cockatoo.

Victoria crowned pigeon – With its deep blue coloring, the Victoria crowned pigeon is among New Guinea's best-known species. It also has a crown of beautiful feathers on its head. In the nineteenth century, the feathers were widely used for decoration.

Australia is also home to birds of prey, such as the wedge-tailed eagle.

Lyrebird
This magnificent bird came close to extinction in the nineteenth century, when it was hunted ruthlessly for its feathers, which were very popular as a ladies' fashion accessory. It feeds on insects, which it finds by hunting around on the ground, underneath leaves.

The cassowary's most distinctive feature is the horny casque, or helmet, on its head.

The black swan is a wonderfully elegant bird, with its plumage of shiny black feathers, its beak edged with red, and its white-tipped wings. It is bred for use as a decorative feature in parks.

Cassowary – This relative of the ostrich lives in the thick forests of New Guinea. The casque on its head helps to break a path through the tree branches when it is in flight.

Bird of paradise – Only the male bird of paradise has the colorful and gaudy plumage. The male lives apart from the female, except for a brief period during the mating season.

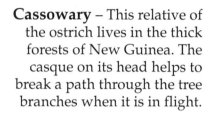

THE AUSTRALIAN PELICAN HAS THE LONGEST BEAK OF ANY BIRD IN THE WORLD—UP TO 20 IN (50 CM) LONG.

There are several kinds of birds in the bird of paradise family. They all have thick and very colorful plumage, with feathers arranged in the most extraordinary fashion.

COCKATOO

Sense of direction
Cockatoos fly long distances every day in search of food, often for many miles. But they can always return to their starting point without difficulty.

The sulphur-crested cockatoo is an Australian parrot, but it is also well known in the west, because it is bred as a domestic bird. It lives in large flocks. Cockatoos can be trained somewhat; the great ethnologist and Nobel laureate Konrad Lorenz owned a cockatoo, which he allowed to fly outdoors. Even when it had flown far away, Lorenz needed only to call out for it and it would immediately return to sit quietly on his arm.

A cockatoo waits its turn to sit on the eggs. Males and females take turns to hatch and feed their young.

Cockatoos are very good at imitating the human voice.

Defending the nest
Although the cockatoo is basically a friendly bird, it will not hesitate to attack any animal that looks as if it may threaten its nest. Cockatoos usually nest in the hollow of a tree trunk, many feet above the ground.

Although it is a different color, the black cockatoo looks like the sulphur-crested cockatoo, and also has a crest that sticks up on top of its head. The two species both live in the forests of eastern Australia.

Chicks – Normally the cockatoo lays two eggs in the nest. The eggs are hatched for about a month, and then the chicks break out of the shells. The chicks' beaks are not black, like those of the adults, but rather are flesh-toned instead.

Sulphur crest – When the sulphur-crested cockatoo is resting, it holds its crest low and close to its head. When it is under attack, it spreads its wings and raises its crest, in an effort to look threatening. Like all parrots, it feeds on fruit and seeds, which it grasps and transfers to its mouth with its talons. It then crushes the shells with its strong beak.

Cockatoos held In captivity live to a very great age. Some have even lived to be over a hundred years old!

159

NEW ZEALAND

Located in Oceania, to the south-east of Australia, New Zealand is made up of two islands: the South Island and the North Island. Its mild, humid climate favors the growth of lush vegetation, which in turn helps animals to live and grow. New Zealand was colonized in the mid-nineteenth century by British settlers. After a period in which native animals were hunted, animal protection laws were introduced and hunting regulated, as in most parts of the world.

Kiwi – This bird, which has an extremely long beak, has become the national symbol of New Zealand. Because its wings have gradually evolved into stumps, the kiwi cannot fly.

New Zealand – Like Italy, the islands of New Zealand form the shape of a boot. New Zealand lies at the *antipodes* of Spain—meaning that it is located exactly on the other side of the globe, diagonally across from Spain, and on the opposite side of the equator—and lies around 1,200 mi (2,000 km) south-east of the Australian coast.

The kea is a typical New Zealand parrot, with a short tail and plumage of a beautiful metallic green. Like other, similar species, it climbs using its legs and beak.

Tiger shark – One inhabitant of the seas around New Zealand that it is best to avoid is the tiger shark. Up to about 30 ft (9 m) long, this shark has spots on its body. It likes to swim in shallow water and around river estuaries. It is considered dangerous to man, and is extremely voracious, and will attack even crocodiles.

THE WORLD'S SMALLEST SHARK IS THE DWARF SHARK, WHICH IS ONLY 6 IN (15 CM) LONG.

The kea owes its name to its distinctive call, which is long and high-pitched, and makes the sound "keeeeah."

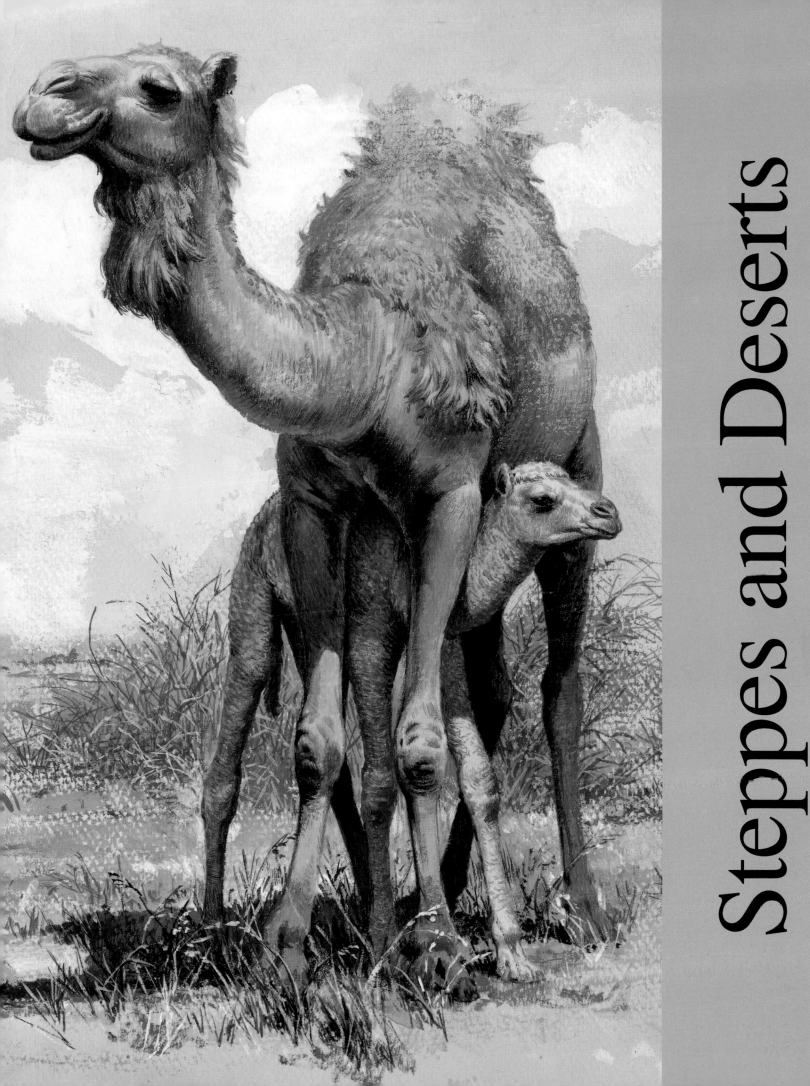

Steppes and Deserts

THE STEPPES OF ASIA

Desolate landscape
The steppe is an area of monotonous, semi-barren plains, where the vegetation is mostly grass. There are no trees, and just a few small patches of different wild grasses. Rivers and streams are also rare.

Climate – Only during the autumn and the spring does enough rain fall to allow the vegetation to briefly grow again. The winters are very cold and the summers, very hot. During these seasons, animals migrate in search of regions where they have a greater chance of survival.

Animal life – Because the region is so poor in resources, animals are scarce. Those that can be found include reptiles, ungulates (hoofed animals), and rodents. Massive swarms of insects migrate in the area in wetter seasons.

1. steppes eagle
2. kiang
3. Bactrian camel
4. Przewalski's wild horse
5. Pallas's cat, or manul
6. great bustard
7. Mongolian gazelle
8. saiga
9. spotted souslik
10. Pallas's sand grouse
11. little bustard
12. bobac

IN THE STEPPES

The steppes are inhabited largely by shepherds and hunters. There are no farmers, because the soil is dry for most of the year, and so crops cannot be grown there.

The people are mostly nomads, who follow the seasonal migrations of animals in search of the little food that the region is able to offer. There are virtually no cars, and people mainly travel around on the backs of horses and camels, the essential means of transport in these regions. There are many herds of wild horses, which are one of the area's great natural resources. The nomads are very skillful at capturing and taming them.

The steppes eagle is not a very big bird. The female weighs around 7 lb (3 kg), the male a little less. Because it lives in areas that are mostly flat and treeless, it spends much of its time on the ground.

The steppes horse is not very tall, but it is has a very tough and sturdy body.

The Bactrian camel is used both as a pack animal and as a means of transport. It is also raised for its wool, its milk, and its meat.

The Bactrian camel is a very tough animal, and can survive at temperatures between 122°F (50°C) and -13°F (-25°C). Camels have been used by humans as working animals since ancient times. The few wild camels that still exist are found in very remote regions, and they are protected by very severe laws.

The blackbuck is a very adaptable animal, and is found over a wide area, although its numbers are falling quickly. It lives not only in the semi-barren regions of the steppes, but also in areas that are rich in vegetation. The male has long horns, which it uses to establish its leadership by pointing them at its opponent. Glands in the blackbuck's face give off a substance that it smears on the ground to mark its territory.

When in danger, the blackbuck flees by making long jumps. This escape tactic usually confuses the predator.

The great bustard is a medium-sized bird that prefers to move by running along the ground, although it can fly perfectly well. It feeds on berries and seeds.

THE HIGHEST TEMPERATURE RECORDED IN THE SIBERIAN STEPPES IS 97°F (36°C). THE LOWEST RECORDED TEMPERATURE IS -90°F (-68°C)

The onager is a wild donkey with a yellowish-brown coat. It spends much of the day looking for food, stopping every once in a while to roll in the dust in an effort to rid itself of parasites. At night, it rests on its side among the bushes.

THE STEPPES OF AUSTRALIA

Vast expanses – Australia is mostly made up of either flat or gently rolling countryside. Some coastal areas have mountain ranges that are quite high and covered with forests of coniferous trees and eucalyptus trees. It is only in these areas that there is a lot of rainfall.

Plants and flowers – In the vast central regions of Australia, the grassy savannah gradually gives way to a large area of steppes, known as scrub, before finally turning into a typical desert or semi-desert landscape.

Animals – The animal life in this region is quite unique. Because the continent of Australia has been cut off from other lands since ancient times, the animal life has not been able to intermingle with that of other continents, and so many species have evolved only in Australia.

1. **carpet python**
2. **little corella**
3. **brush-tail possum**
4. **laughing kookaburra**
5. **frilled lizard**
6. **Australian pelican**
7. **dingo**
8. **yellow-footed rock wallaby**
9. **greater glider**

THE STEPPES OF AUSTRALIA

Due to evolution, Australian mammals are almost all marsupials. Those Australian animals whose young are born fully developed are not marsupials. Because they did not evolve in Australia, and were probably introduced by humans, they are not considered indigenous (or native) to Australia.

The central regions of Australia have a very dry climate. Rain is very rare, and occurs only in the winter and the summer. The seasons are not as clearly divided as in more temperate regions, so there is no large-scale migration of animals looking for favorable habitats. For this reason, the animals that live here are adapted to dry climates, where there is little water.

Laughing kookaburra
This relative of the kingfisher is also known as the laughing jackass because of its distinctive call, which sounds rather like a sort of noisy laughter.

Dingo – Zoologists are convinced that the dingo is not native to Australia, but was introduced in ancient times as a working dog by sailors who arrived here from other countries. The dingo is not much different from most dogs, except that it can't bark; it howls, instead.

The potoroo, or rat kangaroo, is a small marsupial with thick, long fur on its back.

The monitor lizard is a reptile about 51 in (130 cm) long. It eats small reptiles and mammals only every two or three days. It needs little water, and when it does drink, it immerses its head in the water up to its eyes.

The rabbit-bandicoot, or bilby, looks like a small kangaroo. It is completely defenseless, and if attacked, all it can do is try to run away. It digs deep burrows, at surprising speed. Because it feeds on pests such as insect larvae or mice, it is valuable to humans.

Frilled lizard – This animal's most striking characteristic is its ruff—a sort of collar that it opens out like a fan when it wants to frighten its enemies. To make itself look even more terrible, it rears up onto its hind legs, swings its tail, and hisses.

THE RED KANGAROO CAN GROW UP TO 9 FT (2.7 M) LONG FROM HEAD TO TAIL, AND STAND UP TO 6½ FT (2 M) HIGH.

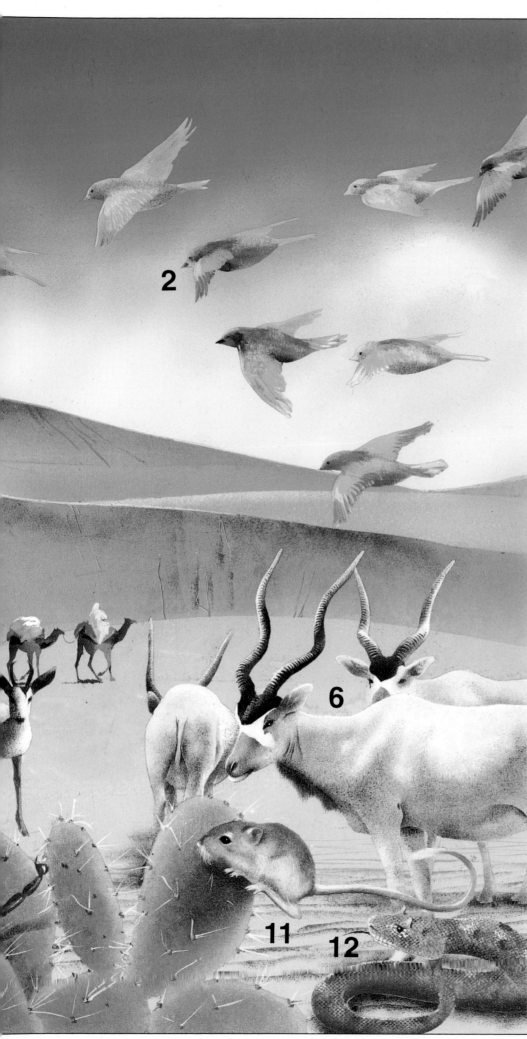

THE SEA OF SAND

Sahara – The world's biggest desert is the Sahara Desert. It lies in North Africa, and covers an area of 3.4 million sq mi (nine million sq km). Here and there, traces of ancient rivers, or *uadi*, can be seen. On the very rare occasions when rain falls, these rivers can sometimes contain water. In some places, water rises from beneath the surface, forming areas rich in plants. These areas are called oases.

Sand dunes – In regions covered with sand, strong winds mold the sand into dunes. This sort of desert is called *erg*. Dunes gradually move over time, like extremely slow moving waves.

Desert of stones – Other regions are covered with crushed stones (*serir*) or with flat rocks (*hamada*) that have been smoothed by the wind and the sand.

1. **white-crowned wheatear**
2. **Sahara sparrow**
3. **dromedary**
4. **fennec**
5. **Dorcas gazelle**
6. **addax**
7. **scolopendra**
8. **mastigure**
9. **and** 11. **Egyptian gerbil**
10. **scorpion**
12. **horned viper**

SANDY DESERTS

The extremely dry climate, the burning hot days, and the icy cold nights certainly do not favor the growth of vegetation, which is limited to a few rare bushes and succulent plants. For this reason, few animals live in these regions.

The Tuareg are a nomadic people that for centuries have crossed the Sahara Desert in long caravans, trading different types of goods.

A dromedary camel calf shades itself from the sun beneath its mother's body. The mother's milk has a very high nutritional value, adapted to the habitat in which the calf must grow up.

Resistance to thirst

A dromedary can go without drinking ten times longer than man. The belief that it has water reserves in its hump is unfounded. What is certainly true, however, is that a thirsty dromedary can drink over 34 gallons (130 liters) of water at a time. This is stored in tissues all over its body.

Cubs – The female fennec gives birth to up to four cubs. Here, a female watches over her two cubs at the entrance to her burrow. Fennecs dig their own burrows and spend the daylight hours inside them.

The fennec is small relative of the fox, weighing only 3.3 lb (1.5 kg). It has huge ears that are 6 in (15 cm) long. Its thick, woolly coat is sandy colored on top and white underneath, and the tip of its tail is almost black.

Nocturnal – The fennec's thick coat is adapted to the cold climate of the night hours, when it emerges from its burrow to hunt for food, which usually consists of insects such as locusts, but may also include other animals and even plants.

The Egyptian gerbil is common in arid (dry) regions, and has highly developed back legs that allow it to make extremely long jumps. Its tail is also very long. The gerbil uses it as a support while it stands erect and studies the surrounding area.

AFRICAN ROCKY DESERTS

Mountains – In the Sahara, there are a number of very high mountain ranges, including the mountains Hoggar (9,571 ft/2,918 m), Tibesti (11,201 ft/3,415 m), and Aïr (7,577 ft/2,310 m). Over a period of thousands of years, the wind has blown the sand against the rocks at such a tremendous speed that the rocks have become round and smooth. Often, sandstorms are created by winds that can travel faster than 62 mph (100 km/h).

Rain – What little humidity there is in this region will often condense forming extremely rare, brief rain showers. This water is very quickly reabsorbed into the ground, or it evaporates.

Vegetation – The special characteristic of the plants that grow in the desert is that they store in their pulpy leaves what little humidity they can obtain directly from the air, rather than from the ground through their roots. Transpiration (the release of water) by plants is virtually non-existent.

1. chameleon
2. East African oryx
3. Barbary sheep
4. blowing viper
5. elephant shrew
6. catfish
7. gecko
8. jackal
9. locust

IN THE ROCKY DESERTS

Whenever a little rainfall allows vegetation to grow, even if only very sparsely, animals immediately gather in the area. Rainfall occurs most often at the edge of the desert, where the first grasses and bushes begin to appear, and in mountainous regions, where water flows briefly in shallow streams at certain times of the year. In these areas, human settlements have arisen, with their crops and their domestic animals. Some species of wild animals are attracted to these regions by the possibility of finding food by living close to humans.

Chameleon
This reptile can change color completely, depending on its surroundings, and also depending on its mood. It will take on different colors according to whether it is excited or frightened.

The hyrax is a herbivore about the same size as a rabbit. Inside its intestines is a little sack that houses the bacteria that help it to digest the tough, fibrous plants it eats.

The oryx is as large as a deer. Its horns are either straight or slightly curved. It can survive without drinking for a period of many weeks, during which it will migrate long distances in search of regions more favorable to its survival.

Open spaces – The regions where the oryx lives offer few hiding places, so it is easy for predators to spot them. They therefore seek the safety of groups, becoming active during the evenings and at night.

The elephant shrew's curious appearance makes it look like a tiny kangaroo. It has a short trunk on its snout.

Servals often catch rodents by sticking their paws down into their burrows or by pouncing on them, an action characteristic to all members of the cat family.

The serval is a medium-sized member of the cat family. It hunts in arid regions, but never strays far from water, which it needs to drink often. Its coat is spotted like that of the leopard, but there is a greater variety in the number, size, and pattern of the dark spots on the serval's coat.

IN LIBYA, A TEMPERATURE OF 136°F (58°C) HAS BEEN RECORDED, IN THE SHADE!

NORTH AMERICAN DESERTS

Hostile environments
In Mexico and in some southern parts of the United States, there are vast desert regions where only a few cactuses and shrubs grow. But many animals can survive even in such a hostile environment.

Natural defenses – The animals that live in these inhospitable regions need to defend themselves from more than other animals. They also need to cope with the burning sun and the lack of water. They survive by using the humidity of the night and the sap from plants.

Nocturnal activity – By day, when the sun scorches the air and the land, only a few animals dare to venture out. At night, however, when the temperature falls, the desert is alive with countless animals in search of food.

1. elf owl
2. bobcat
3. collared peccary
4. western spotted skunk
5. American badger
6. kit fox
7. pack rat
8. gila monster
9. desert tortoise
10. kangaroo mouse
11. prairie rattlesnake
12. roadrunner
13. horned lizard

IN CACTUS COUNTRY

Unconcerned by the spines, a bobcat climbs to the top of a saguaro cactus with its prey.

Many desert regions in the United States have been turned into national parks, where nature is protected by strict laws. Even the cactuses and rattlesnakes may not be harmed. The parks allow the flora and fauna to develop in its own way, with humans allowed only limited access to study and view it. One famous desert area is California's Death Valley, which is 140 mi (225 km) long and between 4 and 16 mi (6 and 25 km) wide. Parts of this region are below sea level, some by as much as 282 ft (86 m).

Pronghorn – If a wolf or a coyote is near, the white hairs on the pronghorn's rump become erect and clearly visible to the other animals in the herd. This warning signal is quickly copied by all the other animals.

Great speed – The pronghorn's chief weapon of survival is its great speed. Able to run at 50 mph (80 km/h), it is faster than any predator. The pronghorn is said to have had a curious interest in the first human settlers to their regions. People could attract the animals simply by lying down and kicking their legs in the air, or by waving a red handkerchief!

The rattlesnake is a species of snake that owes its name to a shell-like formation of scales on its tail, which makes a sharp rattling sound when the snake causes it to vibrate. During the winter, several hundred rattlesnakes often gather together in underground burrows.

Vegetation – Desert plants all have certain things in common: their leaves tend to be rounded and full of pulp, which keeps them humid; they have spines that protect them from hungry and thirsty herbivores; and, to attract pollinating insects, they have brightly colored flowers that open briefly after the rare rainy periods.

The collared peccary looks much like a wild boar. It lives in both wooded areas and in regions where vegetation is sparse. It feeds on plants and small animals, and it has excellent hearing.

The most commonly found cactuses are the opuntia, the mammillaria, the echinocactus, and the cereus.

Elf owl – This small, nocturnal bird of prey eats mainly rodents and insects, and is a very common desert owl. The picture shows a pair of owls that has nested in the cavity of a saguaro, which is the characteristic cactus of the North American desert.

MOUNTAIN LION

This elegant feline (member of the cat family) is also known as the puma or cougar. It has a great ability to adapt. It is found throughout the Americas, in all kinds of habitats. The color of its coat varies slightly according to the region in which it lives, although it is always close to a reddish-brown color. It generally hunts at sunset and at dawn. The mountain

lion is a clever animal. When it tracks down a herd of sheep, it will wait to attack until the middle of the night, when sheep dogs and shepherds are less alert. It is also an extremely agile jumper, and can jump up to a tree branch that is 20-23 ft (6-7 m) off the ground.

The prairie dog was among the mountain lion's favorite prey.
Prairie dogs breed in large numbers, and by preying on them, the mountain lion helped to keep their numbers down. These rodents, however, are now a protected species, after having been nearly wiped out.

Cubs – When they are born, mountain lion cubs have black ears and a coat that is covered with dark spots. Mountain lions lose this coloring the first time they molt, or shed their coat. They then keep the new coloring for the rest of their lives.

Loner – The mountain lion is a very solitary animal. Each individual animal has its own territory, although a female's territory may sometimes overlap with that of a male. Adult mountain lions live together only during the mating season. Cubs stay with their mothers until they are two, when they are old enough to be sent off in search of their own territory.

Tropical Forests

TROPICAL FORESTS AND JUNGLES

The vegetation of the tropical forest is thick and lush. There is a dense layer of undergrowth beneath the tall forest trees, despite the fact that little light filters through the upper branches. The high humidity and frequent rainfall allow all kinds of plants to grow easily. This sort of environment provides the ideal living conditions for countless animals, which find plenty of food. Small and medium-sized animals thrive here, because they are able to move around quickly and easily.

North America – In the Everglades of southern Florida, a large, complex network of swamps, lives the alligator, an animal similar to the crocodile. It is not unusual to see one of these great beasts waddling across the road as you're driving along.

The plants and trees of the rainforest give off abundant water vapor, in a process called transpiration, which in turn produces heavy rainfall.

Aquatic giant – Hippopotamuses spend most of the day in shallow water where they can stay cool, and keep their skin moist and clean. At night they tend to return to land to feed on grasses and plants.

Drinking – After eating, the black panther, a dark version of the leopard, always takes a drink. The black panther weighs around 132 lb (60 kg). During the day, it stays hidden in the thick of the forest. At dusk, it goes off to hunt.

It is not just the water and the land that are home to animals. Trees, too, are often filled with a variety of birds, reptiles, insects, and mammals.

Parrots are among the most colorful and noisy animals to be found in the tropical forest. Their large, hooked beaks, ideal for biting into fruits and seeds, are also used along with their talons for climbing tree trunks. Parrots are thought to be among the most intelligent of all birds.

The gray parrot lives in the forests of western and central Africa.

The sloth is a curious-looking animal, with some equally curious habits. It lives in the forests of South America, attaching itself to the branches of trees with its hook-like claws. It always moves extremely slowly in trees, and when on land, it drags itself along on its chest. Some have been known to live their entire life in the same tree.

Monkeys are excellent climbers, and are common in tropical forests. They generally eat plants and fruits, but will often eat meat, too.

The chimpanzee is considered the most intelligent of all monkeys. It lives in Africa.

NORTH AMERICAN SWAMPS

Ideal habitat – Humans tend to avoid swampy regions, not only because it is hard to build houses and villages there, but also because swamps tend to be places that harbor diseases like malaria. For this reason, animals can live there undisturbed by man. In Florida, a vast region of swamps called the Everglades is home to a wide variety of animals.

The Everglades are home to the alligator, a large reptile similar to the crocodile. Alligators are protected by law, and they can often be seen on the local roads. Some parts of the Everglades are still completely unexplored.

Climate – Because the climate is very humid, the vegetation is thick and lush, providing enough food for a large number of animals.

1. **bald eagle**
2. **roseate spoonbill**
3. **green-backed heron**
4. **brown pelican**
5. **great white heron**
6. **wood stork**
7. **anhinga**
8. **white-tailed deer**
9. **cottonmouth**
10. **alligator**
11. **white ibis**
12. **limpkin**
13. **garpike**
14. **purple gallinule**
15. **European pond tortoise**

PELICAN

The pelican has an unusual body shape and a distinctive beak. It is found on all the continents of the world, with slight differences in shape and size, depending on the region. Pelicans are typically found close to the sea, but they are also found in freshwater regions. They feed on marine animals, especially fish, and have an unusual way of fishing. First, a group of pelicans will splash the shallow water with their wings. This frightens the fish, which head toward the shore in an effort to escape. Here, as they thrash around awkwardly, they are easy prey for the pelicans, which fill their beaks with them. The lower part of the pelican's beak is an elastic pouch, which can stretch to hold many fish at one time. The pelican either eats the fish at its leisure or carries them to its nest.

Size – The pelican is a very large bird. It can be as much as 6 ft (1.8 m) long, with a wingspan of up to 10 ft (3 m). They fly with a light and graceful style. Pelicans hunt for food in groups of various sizes, but they cannot dive very deep.

While it is flying, the pelican holds its neck in a curved position. While swimming, it rests its beak on its neck.

Pelicans are very sociable animals. They live in large communities, even when they are searching for food or building a nest.

The American white pelican spends most of the year in western parts of the United States, Mexico, and Central America. During the mating season, pelicans living further north head toward the south, where the climate is milder and better for rearing chicks. It is almost completely white, except for a few light-yellow patches on its breast and wings.

Feeding its young – The pelican's nest is not a very neat design, and is made from reeds, twigs, and feathers. The adult pelican, either the father or mother, swallows the food before carrying it to the nest. There, the chicks insert their beaks deep inside the parent's beak. This causes the parent to regurgitate the food. Because it is already partially digested, it is much easier for the chicks to eat.

> THE WEIGHT OF A LARGE PELICAN: 31 LB (14 KG).

Pelican chicks
The female pelican lays two or three bluish or yellowish eggs, which it hatches for around thirty days. The chicks are born without any feathers, but their feathers grow within about ten days. The female pelican is slightly smaller than the male.

THE AMAZON FOREST

Great rivers – The Amazon River, at 3,416 m (5,500 km) long, carries more water than any other river in the world. It crosses the huge Amazon plain, which has dense forests and a fantastic variety of animal and plant species.

Plant life – Only the *Indios*, the original inhabitants of the Amazon, know the secrets of the forest. It is hard for people to find their way among the lianas, mosses, and roots. Little light filters through to the ground, the air is dense with vapor, and beautiful orchids grow from the branches, as if suspended in the air.

Animal life – Some Amazonian animals, such as the huge anaconda, are dangerous. Others, such as the slow, peaceful sloth, are harmless.

1. silvery marmoset
2. black-capped capuchin
3. white-faced capuchin
4. Geoffrey's marmoset
5. three-toed sloth
6. green-winged macaw
7. anaconda
8. giant otter
9. peccary
10. opossum
11. jaguar
12. tapir
13. rainbow boa
14. toucan
15. leaf-cutting ant

IN THE AMAZON

Some of the tiniest Amazon monkeys are no bigger than a human hand.

The Amazon is a vast South American pluvial (rain) basin, which was first explored between 1541 and 1542 by Francisco de Orellana. Sadly, each year the advance of civilization brings the destruction of enormous areas of the rain forest, which is exploited for wood or cleared to make way for new farmland. As a result, the animals are forced back into smaller and smaller areas of forest.

Hummingbird – This tiny bird uses its long, curved beak to suck the nectar from the flowers, hovering in the air by flapping its wings at a tremendous speed.

The capybara is the biggest rodent in the world, weighing up to 110 lb (50 kg). It lives close to the water, and will hide in the water if disturbed. While it is on land, its natural enemy is the jaguar. In the water, however, it must be wary of the ferocious crocodile.

Amazon fauna

1. ivory-billed woodpecker
2. parrot snake
3. coral snake
4. blue morpho
5. nine-banded armadillo
6. trumpeter
7. rainbow boa
8. turtle
9. red tegu
10. matamata
11. fer-de-lance
12. red-kneed tarantula
13. leaf-cutting ant

Dense jungle – The sun's rays barely filter through the thick vegetation, which is home to all kinds of animals. Some of these animals, such as the deadly coral snake, are extremely dangerous. There are also animals that may look harmless, but are in fact highly poisonous. These include the poison-dart frogs. An adult male of one such species, the golden poison frog, has enough poison in its small body to kill 1,500 people.

Sloth – The Greek name for this animal means "slow feet," and when it moves, it truly does look as if it is moving in slow motion. Beneath the hairs of its coat are microscopic algae, which grow due to the humidity, and which give the sloth a gray-green coloring that is ideal for hiding among the leaves.

The jaguar is similar to the leopard, but it is bigger and has different markings: dark rings with smaller spots in the center. It is a solitary animal, and since it is not a great climber, it generally hunts on the ground. Once it has caught its prey, it takes it away to an isolated spot, where it can eat at its leisure.

Anaconda – This enormous snake can grow over 30 ft (9 m) long. It often lives in the water, but feeds on land animals as they come to the riverbank to drink.

The jaguar gives birth to two or three cubs. As with all carnivores, when the jaguar cubs are old enough, the mother teaches them to hunt.

Tapir – The most common tapir species in South America is the Brazilian tapir, which lives close to streams and rivers. An excellent swimmer, it can cross very wide rivers and immerse itself in the water to feed on the plants on which it lives.

THE WORLD'S HEAVIEST SNAKE IS THE ANACONDA. ONE SPECIMEN WEIGHED 506 LB (230 KG).

BIRDS OF THE AMAZON

In the dense foliage of the Amazon forest, countless birds live undisturbed. The birds have a wide variety of shapes and characteristics, from the hoatzin, with its red-brown plumage, to the crested cariama, whose legs are better suited to running than its wings are to flying. The quetzal builds its own nest inside a termite nest, without being in the least concerned about the insects. The crested owl, a nocturnal bird of prey, lives in regions that are so difficult to get to that no ornithologist has ever managed to study it. For this reason, little is known about its habits.

The beak of the blue-and-yellow macaw, a brightly colored parrot, is so strong that the macaw can hang from it for several minutes at a time.

The ocellated turkey is an extremely rare bird. All the ocellated turkeys now living in the world's zoos are descended from one mating pair, which successfully reproduced in 1940 in California's San Diego Zoo.

Toucan – With its huge multi-colored beak, which can be longer than its body, the toucan's appearance is unmistakeable. It makes its nest in the hollows of trees, and often occupies an abandoned woodpecker nest.

Sword-billed hummingbird
Flapping its wings at over 50 beats per second, the sword-billed hummingbird can hang suspended in the air and fly at speeds of up to 62 mph (100 km/h). It has a very long beak, which is straight, not curved like those of other hummingbirds.

THE AFRICAN FOREST

Population growth – Africa's population is growing very fast, which means that more and more land is needed for growing crops. As a result, animals are being forced into smaller and smaller areas. Many forests, too, have given way to farmland. Now, most of the remaining forested areas are high up in the mountains.

Camouflage – Whereas the animals of the savannah mostly have a light coloring that allows them to blend in with the parched grassland, jungle animals generally have dark coloring, so that they can move around unseen in the shadows of the trees.

Size – As well as having a different coloring, forest animals are mostly smaller than those living in open areas.

1. leopard
2. cercopithecus
3. python
4. tree pangolin
5. banded duiker
6. okapi
7. hornbill
8. bush pig
9. gorilla
10. African tiger cat
11. mandrill

IN THE FORESTS OF AFRICA

The forests of Africa are found mainly near the equator, where there is not much difference between the seasons, and where the temperature and the level of rainfall hardly change all year. The animals that live there are mostly non-migratory. Unlike animals living in temperate or cold regions, the animals that live in the forests of Africa do not need to migrate in search of better conditions with each change of season.

The hornbill's casque (helmet) and bill are lighter weight than they appear because they are hollow.

The horns of the male bongo can be as much as 3.3 ft (1 m) long. The bongo is a very timid animal that leaves the dense forest only at night, when the white stripes on its coat allow it to blend in with the colors of the moonlit foliage.

Lying in wait – The deep rain forest is filled with animals that lie in wait, motionless, for their prey to pass by. The branches of the trees hide leopards, large snakes, and birds of prey, while crocodiles lie in wait along the muddy banks of lakes and rivers.

Python – Contrary to popular belief, this large, non-poisonous snake is not dangerous to humans. Only exceptionally large specimens would be strong enough to crush a person. Small pythons live up in the trees, while bigger ones usually stay on the ground.

The leopard is an elegant big cat that does not begin to hunt until nightfall. It is an animal that is rarely seen, and often the only way to tell that it has been around is by its tracks, its droppings, or the remains of its prey.

Okapi – Until the twentieth century, few people had ever seen the okapi. A relative of the giraffe, it is very shy and lives in the thick of the forest.

Many of the numerous species and sub-species of cercopithecus have large, brightly colored body parts. This coloration helps members of the same species to recognize one another.

The long-tailed pangolin is covered with a tough shell of overlapping scales. A skillful climber, it feeds on the ants and termites that it finds in the branches and trunks of trees. Sometimes it even manages to destroy the nests of termites, which are built of earth and are extremely strong. Because of the pangolin's very unusual feeding habits, and because it cannot easily adapt to other food, it is difficult to keep this animal in captivity.

The various species of cercopithecus are found close to the water.

The Nile crocodile is enormous, and can be as much as 20 ft (6 m) long. It spends most of the night sleeping in the water. During the day, however, it remains on dry land, basking in the heat of the sun. As well as eating fish, it also attacks animals that come to the water to drink.

Crocodiles are ancient reptiles that existed during the time of the dinosaurs.

Leopard – An adult male leopard weighs about 132 lb (60 kg), whereas leopard cubs can weigh as little as 1 lb (0.5 kg). A female leopard usually gives birth to between four and six cubs.

Hippopotamus – The word *hippopotamus* comes from Greek, and means river horse. The hippopotamus can weigh over three tons.

Marabou – One of Africa's "garbage birds," the marabou lives on dead animals. It is a very big bird, and looks majestic in flight. The female lays two or three eggs at a time in nests built in the trees.

The golden-rumped elephant shrew is a small, insect-eating animal, around 12 in (30 cm) long, with a long, trunk-like nose.

☞ THE WORLD'S MOST POISONOUS SNAKE IS THE BLACK-HEADED SEA SNAKE.

Gorilla – At around 6.5 ft (2 m) tall, the gorilla is the biggest of all the monkeys. Because of its size, many people think it must also be ferocious. In fact the gorilla is a peaceful, often shy, animal, and it is difficult to get close enough to study it in the thick, tangled forest of its natural habitat.

201

HIPPOPOTAMUS

This massive animal spends most of the time in the water, which is its natural element. Because of its tremendous bulk, however, it is not a very skillful swimmer. For this reason it prefers to stay in shallow water, where it can touch the bottom and walk around, rather than swim. The hippo has very flexible ears, a nose equipped with membranes that can be closed up, and bulging eyes. Because its ears, nose, and eyes are positioned high on its head, it can stay semi-submerged while continuing to breathe, keeping a close watch on the surrounding area. If a hippopotamus senses that it is in danger, or that its young are in danger, it can become very dangerous, and will not hesitate to attack whoever or whatever is responsible for the disturbance, whether in the water or on land.

Birth – The mother hippopotamus gives birth to her young either on land or in the water, which offers more protection. If the birth takes place in the water, the new-born hippopotamus immediately surfaces to breathe. Births take place during the rainy season, when the mother can feed herself well, and so produce a plentiful supply of milk.

To suckle its young, the female hippopotamus lies down on her side. The young will even suckle underwater.

Social life – The hippopotamus is not a solitary animal and prefers to live in groups of dozens of animals. Adult males often play with young animals, both on land and in the water. When moving around on land, the hippopotamus will always take the same path. People have been attacked simply because they walked along the path of a hippopotamus by mistake.

Threat – Apart from making a terrifying bellowing noise, a hippopotamus that thinks it is in danger will threaten the aggressor by opening its enormous mouth and showing its extremely long, lower canine teeth. This usually has the desired effect, even though the hippo is a herbivore.

203

CROCODILE

Only one species of crocodile lives in salt water. Crocodiles normally live on the banks of lakes and rivers, in regions where the climate ranges from hot to scorching hot. They are much happier in the water than on land, where they find it hard to move around. They use their tail for swimming, and larger specimens can stay under water for up to an hour. During the hottest part of the day, they lie without moving on dry ground, with their jaws wide open. They do this because they do not have sweat glands, and they get rid of excessive heat through the mucous membrane of their mouth and tongue, rather like dogs.

Young crocodiles feed mainly on fish and birds, but also on insects. Only when they are older are they able to attack larger mammals, which they drag down under the water.

The crocodile does not use its teeth to chew on its prey, only to catch it.

In the water
The crocodile normally moves very slowly, but it will move with lightning speed when attacking its prey.

Eggs – Crocodile eggs are laid in a hole dug into the ground, close to the water's edge. Young crocodiles hatch out of their eggs by breaking the shell with a little horn on their heads. The horn falls off soon after birth.

THE SMALLEST CROCODILE IS OSBORN'S DWARF CROCODILE, WHICH IS ONLY 4 FT (120 CM) LONG.

Enemies – Even this terrible reptile has its enemies: animals that prey on its eggs. The most fearsome is the monitor lizard. When it sights the nest, it digs into the earth with surprising speed, ignoring the female crocodile that is usually standing guard close by. It carries the eggs away to a secluded spot, where it eats them at its leisure.

Like many land animals that live in an aquatic environment, the crocodile's ears, nostrils, and eyes are positioned high on its head, so that they are above the water while it is swimming.

CHIMPANZEE

Language
Chimpanzees have only a few calls, but they also use gestures to communicate with each other. They have a large range of facial expressions, some of which are similar to human expressions.

The chimpanzee is the best known of all monkeys, because of its intelligence and because it can be easily taught. Although it is an excellent climber, the chimpanzee spends most of its time on land, often moving considerable distances from one region to another. It sleeps in the trees, where it is safer from attacks. It is among the few tool-using animals. For example, it will insert twigs into termite nests and eat the insects that cling to them. It will eat a wide variety of fruits, plants, and seeds, as well as eggs and small animals. Chimpanzee troops living in different places will often eat very different foods.

Usually only one baby chimpanzee is born at a time, but sometimes there are twins. Young chimps spend much of their early lives clinging to their mothers.

The strongest males express their power by wrenching plants out of the ground, assuming a threatening posture, or shaking sticks.

Babysitters – Female chimpanzees establish strong friendships with each other, and a mother will often trust her young to another female. Sometimes, this babysitter will take two or three young chimps around with her, and suckle them as well as her own children.

Social life – Chimpanzees live in fairly large communities, but membership in these communities is not as strict as with other species of monkey, such as the gorilla. Chimpanzees will often move from one community to another.

MADAGASCAR

The large African island of Madagascar lies in the Indian Ocean. Only some of the animals found there are the same as those found on the African mainland. Many species are distinct to the island, and are not found in any other part of the world. The hilly country is covered with lush vegetation. This vegetation and the mild climate are the reasons why the island is so filled with animal life. Among the creatures found there are some twenty different species of lemurs, a unique group of animals related to the monkey.

Among Madagascar's characteristic animals are its beautiful, many-colored butterflies.

1. black lemur
2. aye-aye
3. underwing moth
4. mocker swallowtail
5. Verreaux's sifaka
6. mongoose lemur
7. greater hedgehog tenrec
8. fossa
9. ring-tailed lemur
10. dwarf lemur

Lemurs look much like monkeys and also live in the trees. They are very lively, agile creatures with fox-like faces and big eyes that are perfect for seeing at night. Some are so sleepy during the day that they can be caught very easily.

211

THE JUNGLES OF ASIA

Vegetation and climate – The growth of the jungle depends entirely on the amount of rainfall, which is particularly abundant around the equator.

Plant life – Some animals of the Asian jungle, such as elephants, rhinoceroses, and leopards, are also found in Africa. Over hundreds of thousands of years, however, they have developed characteristics that are different from those of their African cousins. Asian elephants, for example, are smaller and less aggressive than African elephants. Other animals, like the tiger, are found only in Asia.

1. gibbon
2. proboscis monkey
3. spectral tarsier
4. python
5. squacco heron
6. king cobra
7. red-necked grebe
8. greater marabou
9. painted stork
10. crocodile
11. mallard
12. mangrove snake
13. jacana
14. archerfish
15. mandarin duck
16. catfish
17. fire-bellied toad
18. moorhen

IN THE ASIAN JUNGLE

The banyan tree, which grows in humid regions, has a unique and curious feature: its branches throw out roots, which grow downward and take root again in the ground. In this way, the tree is able to spread out over a wide area.

Monsoons are winds that blow only in the tropical regions of Asia. They occur on a regular basis, and bring with them a significant amount of rainfall that breathes new life into the jungle and stimulates new plant growth. This climate is also very good for the animals that live in the region. The monsoon season offers ideal conditions to grow and reproduce, because food is plentiful and new plant growth happens quickly. Just like the forest of the Amazon, the jungles of Asia are dense and impenetrable.

The Indian cobra is extremely poisonous. When threatened, it raises its head and spreads its hood to warn that it is ready to strike. The cobra will also spit poison at its attacker.

The gayal is an ox that is raised in Indonesia. By day it grazes freely in wooded areas, and will return to the farm or village at night.

The palm civet is a small nocturnal omnivore, which has learned to live close to humans.

214

The palm civet eats insects, reptiles, small mammals, and even sweet fruit. Although it is well-liked by people because it catches mice, it will sometimes also hunt farm animals.

The Asian elephant has been used for hundreds of years as a working animal. Nowadays, it is increasingly being replaced by machines, but there are still some jobs for which it is irreplaceable.

As with the African rhinoceros, there are very few Indian rhinoceroses left. For this reason, they are protected by very strict laws.

The Indian civet lives mostly on land, but it is also a skillful climber. It hunts for prey from the evening until the early morning.

The Indian rhinoceros, unlike the African rhinoceros, has only one horn, and its body is covered with thick plates of hide. It generally moves slowly, but can gallop as fast as 25 mph (40 km/h).

TIGER

The tiger is an animal that can adapt to many different climates. Some species live in flat, tropical regions, while others live in the mountains, at up to 9,800 ft (3,000 m). Others live in regions so cold that they have developed a layer of fat over 2 in (5 cm) thick beneath their skin to prevent the loss of body heat.

Virtually all jungle animals can be the tiger's victims. It will keep a respectful distance only from big, aggressive pachyderms and from ruminants with sharp horns.

The Siberian tiger can survive at temperatures below -40°F (-40°C).

The hunt – Contrary to popular belief, the tiger is not a highly skillful hunter. The tiger cannot chase its prey for long distances, and hunts by taking its prey by surprise. It must get within 33 to 49 ft (10 to 15 m) of its prey, without being seen, if its final pounce is to stand any chance of being successful.

Litter – There are two, three, or four tiger cubs in a litter. For the first eight weeks the mother feeds them milk only, but she then starts to add solid food. At first, she will leave the cubs alone only for very short periods. Only after six months will she leave them for more than a day to go hunting.

At around six months old, the tiger cub begins to follow its mother around, so that it can learn how to hunt.

Man-eater? – The tiger, like all wild animals, fears humans. But occasionally an old or sick tiger that is unable to capture its usual prey may overcome its natural fear and attack a human being.

Tapir

The tapir is generally regarded as a sort of living fossil. There are just four species of this survivor from an ancient geological period and they are found in regions of the world that are very far apart from each other. The tapir's closest relatives are horses and rhinoceroses. The female is bigger than the male. The tapir's most obvious characteristic is its trunk. An extension of the upper lip, this trunk is very flexible and is used to snatch down the leaves and plants on which it feeds. Asia is the home of the Malayan tapir, which has a very distinctive black-and-white coloring. It might seem that such a distinct coloring would make the tapir very easy to see, but in its habitat, it looks rather like a pile of stones. Young tapirs have striped markings on their coat.

In the wild, tapirs are not sociable animals. It is rare to see more than two or three together. They do not often fight, but when they do, they use their teeth.

Food and habits – Tapirs like to eat leaves, shoots, and fresh branches, which they pull from plants that grow in the water. Tapirs much prefer to live in regions where there is plenty of water, and they are excellent swimmers. Tapirs tend to follow along the same tracks, which eventually grow into pathways, and these usually end with "slides" leading directly into the water.

Defenseless – The tapir's most feared enemies are the big cats and the gavial, a kind of thin-muzzled crocodile. Only very rarely will the tapir try to defend itself against an aggressor. It has few means of defense, and will always try to escape.

Offspring – Young tapirs have yellowish stripes and spots all over their tan-colored coats, like the markings of young fallow deer or boars. When they are about a year old, the young tapirs lose this coloring and take on the characteristic adult coloring, with the white patch that looks rather like a saddle-blanket.

THE MALAYAN TAPIR CAN WALK UNDERWATER ON THE BOTTOMS OF LAKES.

Shape – The tapir is a stocky animal with short legs. It has hardly any neck, so that it sometimes looks as if its head is attached directly onto the main part of its body. The tapir's trunk is very flexible, and gives the animal a very powerful sense of smell. It uses the trunk to hunt around on the ground. The tapir's eyesight, however, is rather poor.

BIRDS OF THE ASIAN JUNGLE

The Chinese magpie is a stunningly beautiful bird.

Up until a hundred years ago, in the days when communications were very slow and difficult, travelers to far-off Asian lands would return home telling tales of birds with beautiful plumage and fantastic colors. And there are indeed many richly colored and beautiful Asian birds, whose feathers were used for many years in western countries to decorate women's hats. Sadly, some bird species were driven to near-extinction to supply the demands of fashion in the West.

Rhinoceros hornbill
The male gathers the materials used to build the nest, but the female gives the nest its final shape. This species has a sort of helmet, or 'casque,' on its beak.

The Indian pitta builds its nest on the ground, or as close to the ground as possible.

Common peafowl are now found in public gardens and parks all around the world. The peacock (male peafowl) has a very long, brightly-colored tail, which it spreads out like a fan. The peahen is brown-colored and quite plain-looking.

The Ocean

LIFE IN THE OCEAN

Over two-thirds of the Earth is covered with seas and oceans. This enormous mass of water is essential to sustain life. Winds carry water vapor from the oceans all around the planet. This humidity then condenses in clouds and falls to the ground in the form of rain or snow, enabling plants to grow and animals to live on land. The seas themselves teem with living creatures. Many of these creatures are too small to be seen with the naked eye, while there are others that are enormous sea beasts, such as the blue whale, the manta ray, and the whale shark, which eat large quantities of microscopic food called plankton.

The jellyfish is 90 percent water. Some species of jellyfish can inflict painful injuries and even cause death in people.

The octopus has eight tentacles. It generally lives among rocky seabeds, and can change color to blend in with its environment.

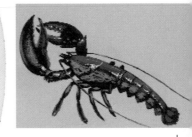

The European lobster has strong claws, which it uses to defend itself against enemies.

This view from space of the Pacific Ocean shows just how vast it is. The Pacific is the biggest ocean on Earth.

Ocean moonfish Because this fish likes to swim close to the surface, many people mistake its protruding fin for that of a dangerous shark. In fact, it is totally harmless.

Loggerhead turtle – An extremely skillful swimmer, the loggerhead turtle feeds mostly on jellyfish and crustaceans. It lives in quiet bay areas, where it lays eggs beneath the sand.

Blue whale
The blue whale is the biggest animal on earth. A female caught in 1947 weighed 190 tons. Our picture shows a blue whale suckling its calf, which at birth can be 26 ft (8 m) long and weigh three tons.

The nautilus is a cephalopod mollusk, like the octopus or the squid.

Murex

This orange mullet has two long barbs, which are organs of touch and taste.

Seaweed – Sea vegetation consists of seaweed, which is a plant with no woody stems. Because it depends on sunlight for its survival, seaweed does not grow in the ocean depths where the sunlight does not reach.

FAR OUT TO SEA

Offshore – In the deep waters far from the coast, there is neither seaweed nor smaller, shallow-water fish or mollusks for animals to feed on. There is only plankton, which is composed of microscopic algae (phytoplankton) and animals (zooplankton), that floats near the surface of the sea. Animals living far out to sea, therefore, either survive by eating plankton, or they are the predators of those plankton-eaters.

Defenses – Far out to sea, where there are no hiding places, only size will stop predators from attacking. This is one of the reasons animals found far out to sea grow to such great sizes. These include the cetaceans (the whale and dolphin family of mammals), and certain large fish, such as sharks, tuna, and swordfish.

Small fish – The ocean's smallest fish use other defense systems. Flying fish can glide for considerable distances above the surface of the water, while sardines and mackerel seek safety in numbers by swimming in very large schools.

1. **flying fish**
2. **dolphin**
3. **Portuguese man-of-war**
4. **jellyfish**
5. **sawfish**
6. **mackerel**
7. **tiger shark**
8. **swordfish**
9. **Atlantic salmon**
10. **hammerhead shark**

CETACEANS

Sea creatures such as whales and dolphins (cetaceans) are the great mammals of the seas and oceans. Millions of years of evolution have given them a shape similar to that of fish, which is ideal for rapid swimming. Unlike fish, however, cetaceans cannot live on the dissolved oxygen contained in water. They must breathe air, and so they must rise to the surface from time to time. Calves are born directly into the water, and their mothers push them to the surface immediately after their birth, so that they can take their first breath. This is a very delicate moment, when the parents must be careful of predators.

Some cetaceans, such as the dolphin, live in relatively shallow water, while others, like the sperm whale, can dive to great depths.

The smallest member of the cetacean family is the dolphin, while the biggest is the blue whale, the largest animal on Earth.

The whale's "spout"
The breathing of a whale looks like a water spout. What we are really seeing is the water vapor in the air condensing, rather like our breath in winter, making a shower of water droplets and mist.

234

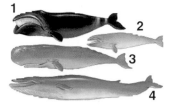

1. Greenland whale
2. Californian gray whale
3. sperm whale
4. blue whale

Food – The Greenland whale, the humpback whale, and the blue whale feed on plankton, which they filter by passing water through a fringe of thick, horny plates called baleen. This filtering stops the whales from eating animals that are too big to be processed by their digestive systems.

1. porpoise
2. Greenland whale
3. humpback whale
4. blue whale
5. sperm whale
6. killer whale
7. beluga
8. narwhal

Humpback whale – Unlike other whales, which live far out to sea, the humpback whale lives quite close to the shore, sometimes appearing in harbors and rivers. Although it weighs 30 tons, it has a playful nature, and loves to make great leaps out of the water.

The sperm whale can be as much as 66 ft (20 m) long. It eats mostly cephalopods such as squid, but it will also eat fish. To catch its prey, it can dive to depths of 3,280 ft (1,000 m), where it finds the giant squid that weighs hundreds of pounds.

Narwhal – Unmistakable because of its long, straight, horn-like tusk, the narwhal is a sociable animal that lives in the cold waters of the Arctic.

The killer whale (or orca) is believed to be a fierce predator by most people. Like all carnivores, however, the killer whale attacks other animals only for food. It has never been known to attack humans.

The dolphin is the natural enemy of the shark. Dolphins have even been known to save shipwrecked sailors from attacks by man-eating sharks.

Dolphin – Because of this mammal's intelligence and its remarkable ability to learn, it is very easily trained.

THE SPERM WHALE CAN GO WITHOUT BREATHING FOR ALMOST TWO HOURS.

Like all cetaceans, dolphins can make a wide range of sounds. Scientists continue to study these sounds to find out if it is a kind of language, like human spoken language.

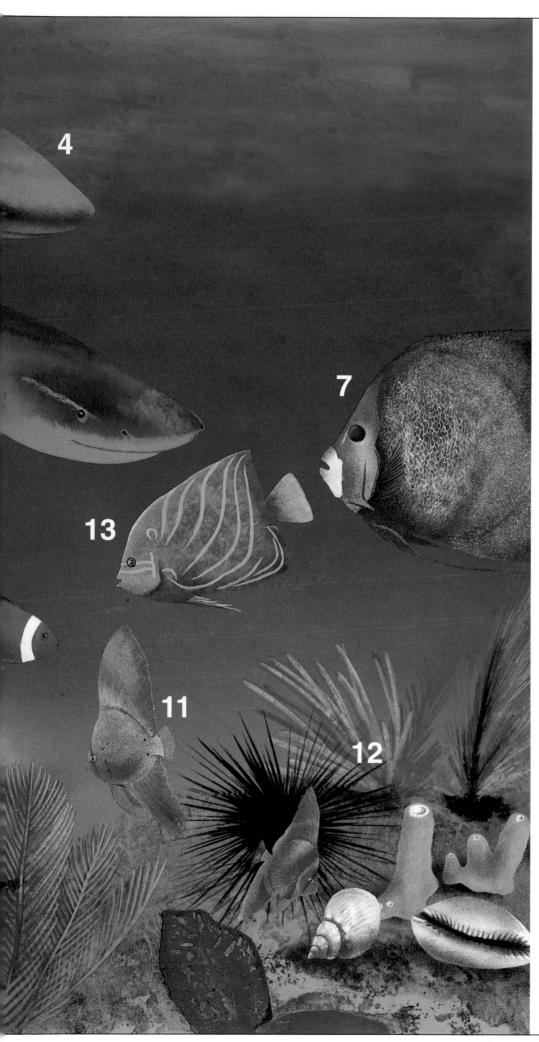

CORAL REEFS

Coral is a colony of animals called polyps. Millions of these polyps attach themselves to each other and to the floors of tropical seas, and produce a hard skeleton. Over a period of many years, these skeletons build up and form an actual barrier, or reef, just off the coast, upon which the ocean waves break. Between the reef and the shore, the sea is as calm as it is inside a harbor.

World of color – The coral reef is an ideal habitat for animals and plants. The sea is calm and the light intense. If you put on a diving mask and look underwater, you will see countless brightly colored, spectacularly beautiful fish swimming among the sea anemones and the starfish.

Deep blue depths – Often the water on the ocean side of a reef suddenly seems much deeper, and darker blue. This is because the in-shore area tends to trap light colored sand, and the churning of these particles creates a distinctive light aqua color.

1. coral
2. banded scat
3. and 10. shrimp
4. shark
5. parrot fish
6. butterflyfish
7. angelfish
8. clown fish
9. giant clam
11. batfish
12. sea urchin
13. ringed angelfish

CLOSE TO SHORE

Ideal habitat – The best conditions for developing marine life are found close to shore. There, the sunlight penetrates into the water, allowing seaweed to grow freely. Seaweed provides food for a number of animals, which in turn provide a source of food for carnivores. The constant wave motion of the water, which is never more than a few dozen yards deep, stirs up the ocean floor and makes it more fertile.

The sea floor can be rocky, sandy, or muddy, and either covered in seaweed or not. The sea floor attracts different animals, depending on its particular characteristics. In sandy regions, for example, we find the sole, which spends its time half-buried in the sand. Rocky areas are home to the octopus, whose coloring makes it almost invisible.

1. **cuttlefish**
2. **rock gunnel**
3. **sea snail**
4. **hermit crab**
5. **scorpion fish**
6. **sea horse**
7. **sole**
8. **nudibranch**
9. **ray**
10. **squid**
11. **sea cucumber**
12. **cowrie**

Starfish, like sea urchins, move by pushing out little stalk-like feet, or *pedicels,* from inside pores in their bodies.

Sea urchins – Whenever you go to the seaside, you have to be very careful not to step on these little creatures. It can be a very unpleasant experience! The mouth of a sea urchin has an organ with five continuously growing teeth, called Aristotle's lantern.

Some sea urchins have short, thick spines, while others have long, thin spines. Their color also varies.

The skeleton of the sea urchin shows its symmetrical, five-sided structure.

The octopus demonstrates a surprising ability to learn, which is a sign of intelligence. Its eight tentacles have suckers on them.

If it is disturbed, the octopus squirts a cloud of black ink that hides it while it escapes.

The cuttlefish is similar to the octopus, although smaller with much smaller tentacles. It has a large flat bone that some people put into bird cages. The birds use it to clean their beaks on.

Collector's pieces

Shells are widely traded, because of their great variety of shapes and colors. There are many shell enthusiasts around the world who collect, buy, and trade them.

The helmet shell is much sought after as an ornament.

The sundial is spiral in form and has attractive colors.

People in some countries use shells as ornaments and musical instruments.

Triton shells can grow very large.

The murex was used in ancient times to extract a purple dye.

The turret shell can have up to 19 spirals.

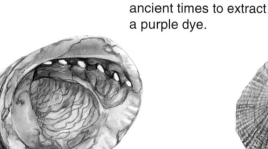

The inside surface of the abalone is iridescent, meaning that it shows different colors of the rainbow that change according to the light or the point of view.

The patella attaches itself very firmly to a rock.

Mussels are bivalve mollusks. This means that they have two separate shell halves (valves). Mussels are farmed intensively, because of their delicious flavor. They feed by filtering the water, retaining those particles that can be eaten.

The cockle is a very common bivalve.

Mussel shells are a beautiful black color with bluish reflections under the light.

The clam has a pale yellow surface, and lives on sandy ocean floors.

CRUSTACEANS

Crustaceans have two pairs of antennae, and most are found in the ocean, although some live in fresh water. Some have large claws, which have a very strong grip. The name crustacean comes from their external skeletons, which are hard, like crusts. During the day, they generally stay holed up in crevices between rocks. At night, they become active and go off in search of food, which mostly consists of mollusks and dead animals.

The lobster lives in seas all over the world, and can weigh as much as 18 lb (8 kg).

The European lobster, like other lobsters, is heavily fished. It is caught in special traps called lobster pots. Unlike other lobsters, it has very powerful claws.

Crabs move with a characteristic sideways manner.

Lairs – Crustaceans have a permanent undersea lair, to which they always return after going out at night in search of food. They must therefore have a good sense of direction. Some, like lobsters, carry out mass migrations, moving slowly over long distances.

The fiddler crab has an extremely large right claw, while its left claw is very small.

1. shrimp
2. starfish
3. crab
4. spiny spider crab
5. hermit crab
6. lobster
7. sea anemone
8. sea urchins
9. shrimp
10. madrepore
11. sea anemone
12. sea anemone
13. crab

The hermit crab protects itself by taking shelter in a gastropod shell.

FROM THE SEA TO THE AQUARIUM

It is easy to keep a freshwater aquarium, but keeping a seawater aquarium is much more difficult. The amount of salt in the water must be kept at the right level. Those who keep an aquarium have much to enjoy, however. Goldfish seem to recognize their owners, and will approach when it is feeding time.

Imperial angelfish
This beautiful sea fish is highly prized, because of its extremely bright coloring. The picture above shows a juvenile specimen.

The top shell feeds on algae and organic waste.

1. ruff	**4.** platy
2. angelfish	**5.** ruff
3. goldfish	**6.** angelfish

The spiny oyster is a bivalve mollusk that spends its life anchored to the sea floor.

The Farmyard

THE FARMYARD

Ancient helpers – When humans were still nomadic hunters, before they learned to cultivate the fields, they used animals, especially dogs, to help them in their daily struggle for survival. Later, humans became farmers, and for many hundreds of years they used animals to help them in their work, until machines arrived to take the place of animals.

Serving a purpose – Some animals were used for their strength. Oxen were used to pull ploughs and carts, while horses made it possible for people to ride quickly from place to place, or were used to pull coaches and carts. Other animals continue to provide their produce: hens provide eggs, cows provide milk, and sheep provide wool. Other animals, such as chickens, rabbits, hogs, and cattle, continue to be raised for their meat. People would have found it hard to develop their human civilization without the help of animals.

1. horse
2. calf
3. cow
4. kid
5. dog
6. duckling
7. chick
8. pig
9. cat
10. rabbit
11. lamb

DONKEYS AND MULES

The young donkey faces a long life of hard work, and can often serve its owner for forty years.

In Egypt, donkeys have been used as a domestic animal since 4,000 BC. They arrived in Europe 2,000 years later. Donkeys are tireless workers. While they are more obedient than horses, they are not as strong. They were used to transport people, to turn millstones, to raise water from wells, and for many other purposes. The offspring of a male donkey and a female horse (or mare) is called a mule, while the offspring of a male horse and a female donkey is called a hinny. These mixed-breed animals are sterile.

Behavior – The donkey is a cautious animal, but it is also very brave. If attacked, it cannot escape as easily as a horse can and so prefers to defend itself with deadly kicks.

Mules – Stronger than donkeys and less sensitive than horses, mules were once used to pull firefighters' carts, because they are not afraid of fire.

PIGS

Hampshire pig

Vietnamese potbellied pig

Poland China pig

The domestic pig is a creature of habit and never strays too far from the place in which it was born and raised. Even in Asia, where they are raised in open spaces, pigs that go off in search of food during the day will return to the village in the evening to spend the night. Surprisingly, the pig is quite close to humans in terms of its physiology (position of internal organs). For this reason, many medical studies are carried out on pigs. In recent years, studies and experiments have looked at the possibility of transplanting the organs of pigs into humans.

Suckling – When it is time for suckling, sows lie on their sides and call to their piglets with a grunting sound. They use the same sound to tell the piglets that the milk has dried up.

UNTIL QUITE RECENTLY, PIGS' HAIRS (OR BRISTLES) WERE USED TO MAKE TOOTHBRUSHES.

Breeds – There are many different breeds of domestic pig, but some breeds are more popular than others. These days, common breeds are the Landrace, which has quite long, white hair through which its pink skin can be seen, and the Large White. Other well-known and common breeds are the Chester White and the Yorkshire.

SHEEP

The sheep is a timid, meek animal. In Europe, sheep are raised for their wool and, to a lesser extent, for their milk, which is used to make special kinds of cheese, such as *pecorino*.

The female sheep is known as a ewe, while the male is called a ram, and the young sheep is known as a lamb. There are many species of domestic sheep that are raised all over the world. There are also a number of wild species, some of which produce highly valued wool. Among these is the urial, which produces very fine, soft wool. Until the Middle Ages, only wool and flax were used to weave fabrics in Europe. Cotton was still unknown, and silk was rare and imported from the Far East.

Wool – Woolen thread is first sold in loose coils known as skeins. The skeins are then put onto revolving looms that wind the wool into balls, which are easier to work with than skeins.

Habits – Sheep spend almost the whole day chewing grass, except for brief periods during which they lie in the shade of a tree. The pregnancy of a ewe lasts for four months, and usually one to three lambs are born, sometimes four.

GOATS

Despite its unpleasant smell, the goat is in fact an animal that likes to keep itself clean. It does not like to be kept in a pen, preferring to run around in the open fields with other goats. Although goats usually feed on grass and shoots, they also adapt easily to the sparse vegetation of areas with dry, barren soil. If they are well treated, goats can provide a plentiful supply of milk.

Goat's milk has a strong flavor and a high nutritional value. It is used to make a strongly flavored cheese.

Characteristics – The coloring of a goat's fur varies quite a lot, and some goats have horns while others do not. Beneath the chin, they have two growths called wattles, and the male goat, or ram, has a long beard.

Habitat – Wild goats normally live in mountainous regions, where they can move around very easily. Their hooves are very tough and grow quickly, and the hard, rocky terrain keeps their hooves short.

CATS

Agility – Almost everybody knows that cats are very agile. Even if they fall from a height of just a few inches, with their backs towards the ground, they can usually flip themselves around and land on their paws. Cats can also jump extremely high.

The Egyptian tabby is generally recognized as the ancestor of modern domestic cats. The ancient Egyptians considered the cat sacred and worshipped a cat-like goddess named Bast. Cats are the only pets that are not social animals, and they see the home as their own territory. Despite its independent nature and its wild character, the cat will sometimes make friends with animals that would otherwise be its natural enemies. These animals include pet dogs, with which it will play and sleep, and other little creatures that live in the same home, such as hamsters, and even little birds. Some people believe that the cat is an unfaithful animal, but in fact its behavior is always quite affectionate to those able to understand it. Not all people understand cats, however.

Defenses – If a cat is attacked by an animal bigger than itself, such as a dog, it will try to avoid a fight by running away. If this is impossible, it will attack by trying to bite and scratch its aggressor. This creates a moment of confusion, which the cat will use to get away. If a mother cat believes her kittens are threatened, however, she will fight to the death.

Siamese cats are highly prized by cat lovers. Their fur is of a light hazelnut color, while their noses, ears, paws, and tails are dark. They have unusual, bright blue eyes.

The tabby cat is among the most common breeds of cat. Its fur is always striped, or occasionally spotted, but the background color varies. Cats have never been bred to serve a certain purpose as dogs have. Instead, cats have been bred to enhance the beauty of certain features, such as the luxurious fur of the Persian, or the blue eyes of the Siamese.

Breeds – There are far fewer cat breeds than there are dog breeds, and these breeds are distinguished only by their coloring, the length of their fur, and partly by the shape of their bodies. One very well-known breed is the Manx cat, which has no tail.

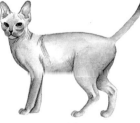

British shorthair tabby

Strays – Because cats are so independent in character, many live wild, without owners. In the wild, male cats often fight with each other to win or to defend hunting territories.

The wildcat is a completely separate species. It is not a domestic cat that has become wild.

Cornish rex

sphinx

bicolor Persian

red Persian

A CAT NAMED TOWSER, WHO DIED AT THE AGE OF 24, WAS RECORDED AS HAVING CAUGHT SOME 28,000 MICE DURING HER LIFETIME IN A DISTILLERY.

HOUSE PETS

Turtles are usually just a few inches long when they are bought, and they can grow to 12 in (30 cm) long when they become adults. They need tanks that are deep enough for them to swim in, with dry areas where they can rest and warm themselves under a heat lamp.

Dogs and cats are not the only animals we call "pets." There are also a number of other common house pets. Generally, these are animals that do not need a great deal of space, such as hamsters, canaries, and goldfish. Even these little creatures need care and someone to look after them. For this reason, it is important to understand their habits and to feed them properly. Taking care of them also includes cleaning their tanks or cages.

Canaries originally came from the Canary Islands, and were introduced to other countries by the Spanish in the late fifteenth century. In the wild, they are not brightly colored. Centuries of crossbreeding and selection have created a variety of multicolored species and other species with strange plumage, such as crests or very thick tails.

Goldfish learn to recognize the people who look after them and can live for many years.

Nest – It is not hard to breed canaries at home, but you must provide them with material for building their nests. When the chicks are born, you must be sure to give the parent birds plenty to eat.

Hamsters love to run around and around on special little wheels that clip easily onto the bars of their cages. These wheels can be bought at your local pet store.

ANIMALS OF THE AMERICAS

The American continent is the only one that reaches from the North to South Poles. Such an enormous range allows a tremendous variety of wildlife.

Class: Mammalia
Order: Carnivora
Family: Ursidae
Genus: Thalarctos
Species: maritimus

polar bear

Class: Mammalia
Order: Pinnipedia
Family: Odobenidae
Genus: Odobenus
Species: rosmarus

walrus

Class: Mammalia
Order: Artiodactyla
Family: Bovidae
Genus: Ovibos
Species: moschatus

musk ox

Class: Mammalia
Order: Pinnipedia
Family: Otariidae
Genus: Callorhinus
Species: ursinus

northern fur seal

Class: Mammalia
Order: Lagomorpha
Family: Leporidae
Genus: Lepus
Species: americanus

snowshoe hare

Class: Mammalia
Order: Artiodactyla
Family: Cervidae
Genus: Rangifer
Species: tarandus caribou

caribou

Class: Mammalia
Order: Artiodactyla
Family: Cervidae
Genus: Alces
Species: alces

moose

Class: Mammalia
Order: Carnivora
Family: Canidae
Genus: Canis
Species: lupus

wolf

Class: Mammalia
Order: Carnivora
Family: Ursidae
Genus: Ursus
Species: horribilis

grizzly bear

Class: Mammalia
Order: Artiodactyla
Family: Bovidae
Genus: Oreamnos
Species: montanus

Rocky Mountain goat

Class: Mammalia
Order: Artiodactyla
Family: Bovidae
Genus: Ovis
Species: canadensis

bighorn

Class: Mammalia
Order: Rodentia
Family: Chinchillidae
Genus: Chinchilla
Species: laniger

chinchilla

Class: Aves
Order: Falconiformes
Family: Accipitridae
Genus: Haliaetus
Species: leucocephalus

bald eagle

Class: Mammalia
Order: Rodentia
Family: Cricetidae
Genus: Dicrostonyx
Species: hudsonius

lemming

Class: Mammalia
Order: Carnivora
Family: Canidae
Genus: Canis
Species: familiaris

husky

Class: Mammalia
Order: Carnivora
Family: Mustelidae
Genus: Mustela
Species: vison

American mink

Class: Mammalia
Order: Carnivora
Family: Mustelidae
Genus: Enhydra
Species: lutris

sea otter

Class: Mammalia
Order: Lagomorpha
Family: Leporidae
Genus: Lepus
Species: articus

arctic rabbit

Class: Mammalia
Order: Cetacea
Family: Monodontidae
Genus: Monodon
Species: monoceros

narwhal

Class: Mammalia
Order: Cetacea
Family: Balaenopteridae
Genus: Megaptera
Species: novae-angliae

humpback whale

Class: Mammalia
Order: Cetacea
Family: Delphinidae
Genus: Orcinus
Species: orca

killer whale

Class: Mammalia
Order: Cetacea
Family: Physeteridae
Genus: Physeter
Species: catadon

sperm whale

Class: Mammalia
Order: Carnivora
Family: Mustelidae
Genus: Mephitis
Species: mephitis

skunk

Class: Mammalia
Order: Rodentia
Family: Castoridae
Genus: Castor
Species: canadensis

beaver

Class: Mammalia
Order: Carnivora
Family: Procyonidae
Genus: Procyon
Species: lotor

raccoon

Class: Mammalia
Order: Marsupialia
Family: Didelphidae
Genus: Didelphis
Species: marsupialis

Virginia opossum

Class: Mammalia
Order: Carnivora
Family: Felidae
Genus: Lynx
Species: rufus

bobcat

Class: Mammalia
Order: Carnivora
Family: Canidae
Genus: Canis
Species: latrans

coyote

Class: Reptilia
Order: Squamata
Family: Crotalidae
Genus: Crotalus
Species: atrox

diamondback rattlesnake

Class: Mammalia
Order: Rodentia
Family: Sciuridae
Genus: Cynomis
Species: ludovicianus

prairie dog

Class: Mammalia
Order: Artiodactyla
Family: Bovidae
Genus: Bison
Species: bison

American bison

Class: Mammalia
Order: Carnivora
Family: Felidae
Genus: Felis
Species: concolor

mountain lion (puma)

Class: Mammalia
Order: Carnivora
Family: Ursidae
Genus: Tremarctos
Species: ornatus

spectacled bear

Class: Mammalia
Order: Rodentia
Family: Caviidae
Genus: Dolichotis
Species: patagonum

mara

Class: Mammalia
Order: Artiodactyla
Family: Camelidae
Genus: Lama
Species: glama

llama

Class: Aves
Order: Falconiform
Family: Cathartidae
Genus: Vultur
Species: gryphus

Andean condor

Class: Mammalia
Order: Artiodactyla
Family: Camelidae
Genus: Lama
Species: vicugna

vicuña

Class: Mammalia
Order: Carnivora
Family: Felidae
Genus: Felis
Species: yaguaroundi

jaguarundi

Class: Mammalia
Order: Edentata
Family: Dasypodidae
Genus: Priodontes
Species: giganteus

giant armadillo

jaguar

Class: Mammalia
Order: Carnivora
Family: Felidae
Genus: Panthera
Species: onca

blue-and-yellow macaw

Class: Aves
Order: Psittaciformes
Family: Psittacidae
Genus: Ara
Species: ararauna

collared peccary

Class: Mammalia
Order: Artiodactyla
Family: Tayassuidae
Genus: Tayassu
Species: tajacu

ocellated turkey

Class: Aves
Order: Galliformes
Family: Meleagrididae
Genus: Meleagris
Species: ocellata

giant anteater

Class: Mammalia
Order: Edentata
Family: Myrmecophagidae
Genus: Myrmecophaga
Species: tridactyla

two-toed sloth

Class: Mammalia
Order: Edentata
Family: Bradypodidae
Genus: Choloepus
Species: didactylus

Brazilian tapir

Class: Mammalia
Order: Perissodactyla
Family: Tapiridae
Genus: Tapirus
Species: terrestris

Class: Aves
Order: Apodiformes
Family: Trochilidae
Genus: Ensifera
Species: ensifera

sword-billed hummingbird

ANIMALS OF EUROPE

Over the past few centuries, Europe has undergone many changes in its natural habitats because of tremendous growth in its human population. Many species of animals have become extinct as a result.

Class: Mammalia
Order: Carnivora
Family: Mustelidae
Genus: Gulo
Species: gulo

wolverine

Class: Aves
Order: Charadriiformes
Family: Alcidae
Genus: Fratercula
Species: artica

puffin

Class: Aves
Order: Anseriformes
Family: Anatidae
Genus: Anser
Species: caerulescens

snow goose

Class: Aves
Order: Charadriiformes
Family: Laridae
Genus: Sterna
Species: paradisaea

arctic tern

Class: Mammalia
Order: Pinnipedia
Family: Phocidae
Genus: Pagophilus
Species: groenlandicus

harp seal

Class: Mammalia
Order: Carnivora
Family: Mustelidae
Genus: Mustela
Species: erminea

ermine

Class: Mammalia
Order: Artiodactyla
Family: Cervidae
Genus: Rangifer
Species: tarandus

reindeer

Class: Aves
Order: Falconiformes
Family: Accipitridae
Genus: Aquila
Species: chrysaetos

golden eagle

Class: Mammalia
Order: Artiodactyla
Family: Bovidae
Genus: Ovis
Species: musimon

mouflon

Class: Aves
Order: Galliformes
Family: Tetraonidae
Genus: Tetrao
Species: urogallus

capercaillie

Class: Mammalia
Order: Carnivora
Family: Canidae
Genus: Canis
Species: familiaris

Saint Bernard

Class: Mammalia
Order: Artiodactyla
Family: Bovidae
Genus: Capra
Species: ibex

alpine ibex

Class: Mammalia
Order: Artiodactyla
Family: Bovidae
Genus: Rupicapra
Species: rupicapra

chamois

Class: Mammalia
Order: Rodentia
Family: Sciuridae
Genus: Marmota
Species: marmota

alpine marmot

Class: Aves
Order: Falconiformes
Family: Falconidae
Genus: Falco
Species: peregrinus

peregrine falcon

Class: Reptilia
Order: Serpentis
Family: Viperidae
Genus: Vipera
Species: aspis

viper, or asp

Class: Mammalia
Order: Carnivora
Family: Mustelidae
Genus: Meles
Species: meles

European badger

Class: Mammalia
Order: Artiodactyla
Family: Cervidae
Genus: Capreolus
Species: capreolus

roe deer

Class: Mammalia
Order: Lagomorpha
Family: Leporidae
Genus: Lepus
Species: europaeus

brown hare

Class: Mammalia
Order: Carnivora
Family: Felidae
Genus: Felis
Species: sylvestris

wild cat

Class: Aves
Order: Anseriformes
Family: Anatidae
Genus: Anas
Species: platyrhynchos

mallard

Class: Mammalia
Order: Carnivora
Family: Ursidae
Genus: Ursus
Species: arctos

brown bear

Class: Mammalia
Order: Insectivora
Family: Erinaceidae
Genus: Erinaceus
Species: europaeus

hedgehog

Class: Mammalia
Order: Carnivora
Family: Viverridae
Genus: Genetta
Species: genetta

genet

Class: Mammalia
Order: Rodentia
Family: Hystricidae
Genus: Hystrix
Species: cristata

porcupine

Class: Mammalia
Order: Carnivora
Family: Mustelidae
Genus: Martes
Species: foina

beech marten

Class: Mammalia
Order: Rodentia
Family: Gliridae
Genus: Glis
Species: glis

dormouse

Class: Mammalia
Order: Carnivora
Family: Mustelidae
Genus: Martes
Species: nivalis

weasel

Class: Mammalia
Order: Artiodactyla
Family: Cervidae
Genus: Cervus
Species: elaphus

red deer

Class: Mammalia
Order: Artiodactyla
Family: Suidi
Genus: Sus
Species: scrofa

wild boar

Class: Aves
Order: Ciconiformes
Family: Ciconidae
Genus: Ciconia
Species: ciconia

white stork

Class: Mammalia
Order: Rodentia
Family: Sciuridae
Genus: Sciurus
Species: vulgaris

red squirrel

red fox

Class: Mammalia
Order: Carnivora
Family: Canidae
Genus: Vulpes
Species: vulpes

Class: Mammalia
Order: Carnivora
Family: Mustelidae
Genus: Martes
Species: martes

pine marten

loggerhead sea turtle

Class: Reptilia
Order: Testudinata
Family: Chelonidae
Genus: Caretta
Species: caretta

Class: Mammalia
Order: Carnivora
Family: Mustelidae
Genus: Lutra
Species: lutra

otter

fin whale

Class: Mammalia
Order: Cetacea
Family: Balaenopteridae
Genus: Balaenoptera
Species: physalus

Class: Mammalia
Order: Primates
Family: Cercopithecidae
Genus: Macaca
Species: sylvana

dolphin

Class: Mammalia
Order: Cetacea
Family: Delphinidae
Genus: Tursiops
Species: truncatus

Barbary ape

ANIMALS OF ASIA

The wildlife of Asia includes many different species that have adapted to the continent's diverse environmental conditions.

arctic fox

Class: Mammalia
Order: Carnivora
Family: Canidae
Genus: Alopex
Species: lagopus

white polar wolf

Class: Mammalia
Order: Carnivora
Family: Canidae
Genus: Canis
Species: lupus

Class: Aves
Order: Galliformes
Family: Tetraonidae
Genus: Lagopus
Species: lagopus

willow ptarmigan

souslik

Class: Mammalia
Order: Rodentia
Family: Sciuridae
Genus: Citellus
Species: citellus

Class: Mammalia
Order: Artiodactyla
Family: Bovidae
Genus: Saiga
Species: tatarica

saiga

whooper swan

Class: Aves
Order: Anseriformes
Family: Anatidae
Genus: Cygnus
Species: cygnus

Class: Mammalia
Order: Artiodactyla
Family: Bovidae
Genus: Ovis
Species: orientalis

argali

markhor

Class: Mammalia
Order: Artiodactyla
Family: Bovidae
Genus: Capra
Species: falconeri

yak

Class: Mammalia
Order: Artiodactyla
Family: Bovidae
Genus: Bos
Species: mutus

pika

Class: Mammalia
Order: Lagomorpha
Family: Ochotonidae
Genus: Ochotona
Species: hyperborea

musk deer

Class: Mammalia
Order: Artiodactyla
Family: Cervidae
Genus: Moschus
Species: moschiferus

snow leopard

Class: Mammalia
Order: Carnivora
Family: Felidae
Genus: Felis
Species: uncia

red panda

Class: Mammalia
Order: Carnivora
Family: Procyonidae
Genus: Ailurus
Species: fulgens

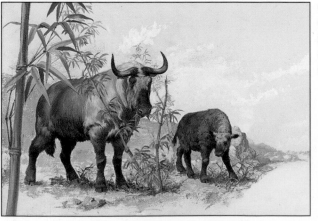

takin

Class: Mammalia
Order: Artiodactyla
Family: Bovidae
Genus: Budorcas
Species: taxicolor

Lady Amherst pheasant

Class: Aves
Order: Galliformes
Family: Phasianidae
Genus: Chrysolophus
Species: amherstiae

blackbuck, or Indian antelope

Class: Mammalia
Order: Artiodactyla
Family: Bovidae
Genus: Antilope
Species: cervicapra

Class: Mammalia
Order: Carnivora
Family: Ursidae
Genus: Ailuropoda
Species: melanoleuca

giant panda

langur

Class: Mammalia
Order: Primates
Family: Cercopithecidae
Genus: Presbytis
Species: senex

Class: Mammalia
Order: Artiodactyla
Family: Bovidae
Genus: Tetracerus
Species: quadricornis

four-horned antelope

Bactrian camel

Class: Mammalia
Order: Artiodactyla
Family: Camelidae
Genus: Camelus
Species: bactrianus

Class: Mammalia
Order: Artiodactyla
Family: Equidae
Genus: Equus
Species: hemionus
onager

onager

muntjac

Class: Mammalia
Order: Artiodactyla
Family: Cervidae
Genus: Muntiacus
Species: muntjak

Class: Mammalia
Order: Primates
Family: Cercopithecidae
Genus: Macaca
Species: fuscata

Japanese macaque

Class: Mammalia
Order: Carnivora
Family: Ursidae
Genus: Helarctos
Species: malayanus

Malay bear, or sun bear

Class: Mammalia
Order: Primates
Family: Pongidae
Genus: Pongo
Species: pygmaeus

orangutang

Class: Mammalia
Order: Primates
Family: Lorisidae
Genus: Loris
Species: gracilis

slender loris

Class: Mammalia
Order: Carnivora
Family: Viverridae
Genus: Paradoxurus
Species: hermaphroditus

palm civet

Class: Aves
Order: Coraciformes
Family: Bucerotidae
Genus: Buceros
Species: rhinoceros

rhinoceros hornbill

Class: Mammalia
Order: Perissodactyla
Family: Tapiridae
Genus: Tapirus
Species: indicus

Malayan tapir

Class: Mammalia
Order: Carnivora
Family: Felidae
Genus: Panthera
Species: pardus

black panther

Class: Mammalia
Order: Artiodactyla
Family: Bovidae
Genus: Bibos
Species: frontalis

gayal

Indian elephant

Class: Mammalia
Order: Proboscidae
Family: Elephantidae
Genus: Elephas
Species: maximus

tiger

Class: Mammalia
Order: Carnivora
Family: Felidae
Genus: Panthera
Species: tigris

common peafowl

Class: Aves
Order: Galliformes
Family: Phasianidae
Genus: Pavo
Species: cristatus

Indian rhinoceros

Class: Mammalia
Order: Perissodactyla
Family: Rhinocerotidae
Genus: Rhinoceros
Species: unicornis

crested wild boar

Class: Mammalia
Order: Artiodactyla
Family: Suidae
Genus: Sus
Species: cristatus

pygmy hog

Class: Mammalia
Order: Artiodactyla
Family: Suidae
Genus: Sus
Species: salvanius

viverrine or fishing cat

Class: Mammalia
Order: Carnivora
Family: Felidae
Genus: Felis
Species: viverrina

Indian civet

Class: Mammalia
Order: Carnivora
Family: Viverridae
Genus: Viverra
Species: zibetha

ANIMALS OF AFRICA

African animals are among the most well known in the world. Public concern about their survival has led to the enactment of legislation and the creation of vast wildlife parks for their protection.

Class: Mammalia
Order: Artiodactyla
Family: Camelidae
Genus: Camelus
Species: dromedarius

dromedary

Class: Mammalia
Order: Carnivora
Family: Canidae
Genus: Fennecus
Species: zerda

fennec

Class: Mammalia
Order: Carnivora
Family: Felidae
Genus: Acinonyx
Species: jubatus

cheetah

Class: Reptilia
Order: Crocodilia
Family: Crocodylidae
Genus: Crocodylus
Species: niloticus

Nile crocodile

Class: Aves
Order: Gruiformes
Family: Gruidae
Genus: Balearica
Species: pavonina

crowned crane

Class: Mammalia
Order: Carnivora
Family: Felidae
Genus: Panthera
Species: pardus

leopard

Class: Mammalia
Order: Carnivora
Family: Felidae
Genus: Panthera
Species: leo

lion

Class: Mammalia
Order: Artiodactyla
Family: Suidae
Genus: Phacochoerus
Species: aethiopicus

warthog

Class: Mammalia
Order: Carnivora
Family: Viverridae
Genus: Ichneumoania
Species: albicauda

white-tailed mongoose

Class: Mammalia
Order: Artiodactyla
Family: Giraffidae
Genus: Giraffa
Species: camelopardalis

giraffe

Class: Mammalia
Order: Artiodactyla
Family: Bovidae
Genus: Gazella
Species: thomsonii

Thomson's gazelle

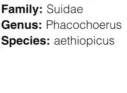

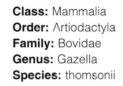

Class: Mammalia
Order: Carnivora
Family: Felidae
Genus: Felis
Species: serval

serval

Class: Mammalia
Order: Perissodactyla
Family: Rhinocerotidae
Genus: Diceros
Species: bicornis

black rhinoceros

Class: Mammalia
Order: Primates
Family: Pongidae
Genus: Pan
Species: troglodytes

chimpanzee

Class: Mammalia
Order: Proboscidea
Family: Elephantidae
Genus: Loxodonta
Species: africana

African elephant

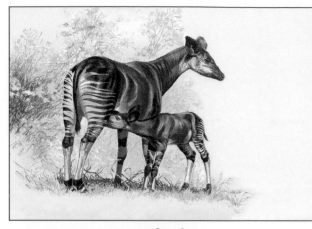

okapi

Class: Mammalia
Order: Artiodactyla
Family: Giraffidae
Genus: Okapia
Species: johnstoni

gorilla

Class: Mammalia
Order: Primates
Family: Pongidae
Genus: Gorilla
Species: gorilla

hippopotamus

Class: Mammalia
Order: Artiodactyla
Family: Hippopotamidae
Genus: Hippopotamus
Species: amphibius

long-tailed pangolin

Class: Mammalia
Order: Pholidota
Family: Manidae
Genus: Manis
Species: tetradactyla

bat-eared fox

Class: Mammalia
Order: Carnivora
Family: Canidae
Genus: Otocyon
Species: megalotis

black-backed jackal

Class: Mammalia
Order: Carnivora
Family: Canidae
Genus: Canis
Species: mesomelas

oryx

Class: Mammalia
Order: Artiodactyla
Family: Bovidae
Genus: Oryx
Species: gazella

zebu

Class: Mammalia
Order: Artiodactyla
Family: Bovidae
Genus: Bos
Species: indicus

Class: Aves
Order: Pelecaniformes
Family: Pelecanidae
Genus: Pelecanus
Species: rufescens

pink-backed pelican

Grant's zebra

Class: Mammalia
Order: Artiodactyla
Family: Equidae
Genus: Equus
Species: burchelli granti

Class: Mammalia
Order: Artiodactyla
Family: Bovidae
Genus: Connochaetes
Species: taurinus

brindled gnu

impala

Class: Mammalia
Order: Artiodactyla
Family: Bovidae
Genus: Aepyceros
Species: melampus

Class: Mammalia
Order: Artiodactyla
Family: Bovidae
Genus: Tragelaphus
Species: strepsiceros

greater kudu

ostrich

Class: Aves
Order: Struthioniformes
Family: Struthionidae
Genus: Struthio
Species: camelus

Class: Mammalia
Order: Artiodactyla
Family: Bovidae
Genus: Syncerus
Species: caffer

African buffalo

Class: Aves
Order: Passeriformes
Family: Nectariniidae
Genus: Anthreptes
Species: platurus

sunbird

ANIMALS OF OCEANIA AND ANTARCTICA

The animals that have evolved in Oceania and Antarctica are quite distinct from those found on the other continents. Mammals originating in Australia, for example, are all marsupials.

bird of paradise

Class: Aves
Order: Passeriformes
Family: Paradisaeidae
Genus: Paradisaea
Species: apoda

spotted cuscus

Class: Mammalia
Order: Marsupialia
Family: Phalangeridae
Genus: Phalanger
Species: maculatus

Class: Aves
Order: Columbiformes
Family: Columbidae
Genus: Goura
Species: victoria

crowned pigeon

frilled lizard

Class: Reptilia
Order: Squamata
Family: Agamidae
Genus: Chlamydosaurus
Species: kingii

Class: Mammalia
Order: Marsupialia
Family: Phalangeridae
Genus: Petaurus
Species: breviceps

sugar glider

spiny anteater

Class: Mammalia
Order: Monotremata
Family: Tachyglossidae
Genus: Tachyglossus
Species: aculeatus

Class: Mammalia
Order: Carnivora
Family: Canidae
Genus: Canis
Species: familiaris dingo

dingo

Class: Mammalia
Order: Marsupialia
Family: Paramelidae
Genus: Macrotis
Species: lagotis

rabbit-bandicoot, or bilby

Class: Mammalia
Order: Marsupialia
Family: Macropodidae
Genus: Dendrolagus
Species: lumholtzi

Lumholtz's tree kangaroo

Class: Aves
Order: Falconiformes
Family: Accipitridae
Genus: Aquila
Species: audax

wedge-tailed eagle

Class: Mammalia
Order: Maruspialia
Family: Phascolarctidae
Genus: Phascolarctos
Species: cinereus

koala

Class: Mammalia
Order: Marsupialia
Family: Dasyuridae
Genus: Satanellus
Species: albopunctatus

native cat

Class: Aves
Order: Passeriformes
Family: Menuridae
Genus: Menura
Species: novaehollandiae

lyrebird

Class: Aves
Order: Anseriformes
Family: Anatidae
Genus: Cygnus
Species: atratus

black swan

Class: Aves
Order: Casuariiformes
Family: Dromaiidae
Genus: Dromaius
Species: novaehollandiae

emu

numbat

Class: Mammalia
Order: Marsupialia
Family: Myrmecobiidae
Genus: Myrmecobius
Species: fasciatus

great gray kangaroo

Class: Mammalia
Order: Marsupialia
Family: Macropodidae
Genus: Macropus
Species: giganteus

cassowary

Class: Aves
Order: Casuariiformes
Family: Casuariidae
Genus: Casuarius
Species: casuarius

Class: Mammalia
Order: Monotremata
Family: Ornithorhynchidae
Genus: Ornithorhynchus
Species: anatinus

duck-billed platypus

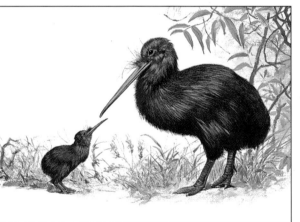

kiwi

Class: Aves
Order: Apterygiformes
Family: Apterygidae
Genus: Apteryx
Species: australis

Class: Pisces
Order: Elasmobranch
Family: Squaloidea
Genus: Galeocerdo
Species: cuvieri

tiger shark

wombat

Class: Mammalia
Order: Marsupialia
Family: Phascolomidae
Genus: Vombatus
Species: ursinus

Class: Mammalia
Order: Marsupialia
Family: Dasyuridae
Genus: Thylacinus
Species: cynocephalus

Tasmanian wolf

Class: Mammalia
Order: Marsupialia
Family: Phalangeridae
Genus: Trichosurus
Species: vulpecula

brush-tail opossum

Tasmanian devil

Class: Mammalia
Order: Marsupiali
Family: Dasyuridae
Genus: Sarcophilus
Species: harrisii

Class: Aves
Order: Psittaciformes
Family: Psittacidae
Genus: Cacatua
Species: galerita

sulphur-crested cockatoo

kea

Class: Aves
Order: Psittaciformes
Family: Psittacidae
Genus: Nestor
Species: notabilis

Class: Mammalia
Order: Pinnipedia
Family: Phocidae
Genus: Mirounga
Species: leonina

southern elephant seal

wandering albatross

Class: Aves
Order: Procellariiformes
Family: Diomedeidae
Genus: Diomedea
Species: exulans

Class: Aves
Order: Sphenisciformes
Family: Spheniscidae
Genus: Aptenodytes
Species: patagonica

king penguin

leopard seal

Class: Mammalia
Order: Pinnipedia
Family: Phocidae
Genus: Hydrurga
Species: leptomyx

DOMESTIC AND FARM ANIMALS

Since ancient times people have raised animals that have helped them in their daily work or that have provided them with food. Domestic and farm animals found throughout the world are very similar. Slight differences are due to the various environments in which they live.

Class: Aves
Order: Galliformes
Family: Phasianidae
Genus: Gallus
Species: gallus

chicken

Class: Aves
Order: Galliformes
Family: Numididae
Genus: Numida
Species: meleagris

guinea fowl

Class: Aves
Order: Galliformes
Family: Meleagrididae
Genus: Meleagris
Species: gallopavo

turkey

Class: Mammalia
Order: Artiodactyla
Family: Bovidae
Genus: Bos
Species: taurus

cow

Class: Mammalia
Order: Perissodactyla
Family: Equidae
Genus: Equus
Species: caballus

horse

Class: Mammalia
Order: Perissodactyla
Family: Equidae
Genus: Equus
Species: asinus

donkey

Class: Mammalia
Order: Artiodactyla
Family: Suidae
Genus: Sus
Species: scrofa

pig

Class: Mammalia
Order: Artiodactyla
Family: Bovidae
Genus: Ovis
Species: aries

sheep

goat

Class: Mammalia
Order: Artiodactyla
Family: Bovidae
Genus: Capra
Species: hircus

Class: Mammalia
Order: Lagomorpha
Family: Leporidae
Genus: Oryctolagus
Species: cuniculus

Class: Mammalia
Order: Rodentia
Family: Muridae
Genus: Mus
Species: musculus

rabbit

mouse

Class: Mammalia
Order: Rodentia
Family: Caviidae
Genus: Cavia
Species: porcellus

Class: Aves
Order: Anseriformes
Family: Anatidae
Genus: Anas
Species: platyrhynchos

guinea pig

duck

Class: Aves
Order: Anseriformes
Family: Anatidae
Genus: Anser
Species: anser

Class: Aves
Order: Anseriformes
Family: Anatidae
Genus: Cygnus
Species: olor

goose

swan

Class: Aves
Order: Passeriformes
Family: Ploceidae
Genus: Passer
Species: domesticus

Class: Aves
Order: Passeriformes
Family: Hirundinidae
Genus: Hirundo
Species: rusticus

sparrow

swallow

Class: Aves
Order: Columbiformes
Family: Columbidae
Genus: Columba
Species: livia

Class: Reptilia
Order: Testudines
Family: Testudinidae
Genus: Testudo
Species: graeca

pigeon

tortoise

Class: Mammalia
Order: Carnivora
Family: Canidae
Genus: Canis
Species: familiaris

Class: Mammalia
Order: Carnivora
Family: Felidae
Genus: Felis
Species: domesticus

dog

cat

Class: Osteichthyes
Order: Cypriniformes
Family: Cyprinidae
Genus: Carassius
Species: auratus

Class: Aves
Order: Passeriformes
Family: Fringillidae
Genus: Serinus
Species: canarius

goldfish

canary

Dictionaries

Dictionary of Fish

Adipose Fin: A type of dorsal fin that is fleshy, rich in fat, flexible, lacks spiny rays, and is characteristic of certain fish such as salmonids (salmon, trout, etc.).

Anadromous: A word used to describe animals, especially fish, that migrate from the sea to rivers to spawn. Among the best-known anadromous fish are the salmon and sturgeon. From the Greek: *anà* = upwards, and *dromos* = running

sea bass

Aquarium Keeping: The discipline governing the construction and maintenance of aquariums and the life forms contained in them.

Aquarium: A container, usually glass, filled with water, with water filtration equipment, which provides an environment for fish in which they can live and reproduce. Also can contain aquatic plants and other organisms. An aquarium can also be a building that displays a living collection of fish in tanks in which their natural environment is recreated.

Archerfish: This member of the family Toxotidae lives in the brackish marshes of Oceania. Its main characteristic is its unusual hunting method: it lies in wait just below the surface of the water, then it knocks insects resting on leaves into the water by squirting them with a jet of water.

Barbel: A slender extension, like a beard, near the mouth of certain bottom fishes.

Batfish: This bony fish of the family Ogcocephalidae lives in warm and temperate waters worldwide. These bottom-dwellers are named for their wide, flattened body and modified pectoral fins, which extend like arms at an angle from the head.

Beadlet Anemone: The common name for *Actinia equina*.

Blenny: The name given to various fishes of the family Blennidae. Blennies are found mostly in tropical and warm temperate seas, but there are freshwater species as well. Blennies are typically deep-sea fish and known for the large amounts of mucus covering their skin.

archerfish

flying fish

Butterflyfish: A marine fish belonging to the Chaetondontidae family. This fish lives in pairs in the Indian and Pacific Oceans along coral reefs, where it feeds by extracting its food from cracks in the rocks with its elongated jaw called a rostrum. It grows to a length of about 6 in (16 cm).

Catadromous: A word to describe animals, especially fish, that migrate from rivers towards the sea to spawn. Eels are among the most common catadromous fish. From Ancient greek *catà* = downwards and *dromos* = running

Cichlids: A family of freshwater tropical fish that includes about 900 species distributed through Central America, South America, Africa, and part of Asia. Cichlids, especially those found in the large African lakes, are greatly appreciated by aquarium enthusiasts the world over for their extraordinary variety of colors, which are similar to brilliant colors of fish found around coral reefs in salt water.

Clownfish: The name given to various species of marine fish of the family Pomacentridae found in the tropical waters of the Indian and Pacific Oceans. Its name derives from its coloring, which resembles a circus clown's make-up. A characteristic of all clownfish is its symbiotic relationship (that is, a mutually beneficial living arrangement) with sea anemones and their apparent immunity to the poison in the anemone's stinger cells.

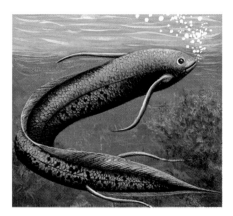

protopterus

Cuttlefish: Like the octopus, this cephalopod mollusk has eight tentacles, two of which are used only in the mating ritual. The cuttlefish has a sack-shaped body supported by an internal shell, or cuttle-bone. It can change color quickly in much the same way as the octopus. This fish lives in sandy depths and, when in danger, discharges a cloud of brownish-black ink. At one time this ink was used for writing.

Dory, or John Dory: A bony fish of the family Zeidae, the dory lives in the open waters of the western Atlantic Ocean, the Mediterranean Sea, and the Black Sea, growing to 20 in (50 cm) in length. According to legend, the yellow-ringed dark spot located in the center of its body is the mark made by Saint Peter when he grasped the fish to remove a gold coin from its mouth.

Eel: A predominately nocturnal, bony fish with a snake-like body, the eel spends most of its life (8 to 18 years) in rivers or brackish water, but migrates

from 2,500 to 4,300 miles (4,000 to 7,000 km) towards the sea to spawn (a catadromous fish). Most of the eels living in Europe's rivers go to a part of the Atlantic Ocean known as the Sargasso Sea to spawn. Here the adults (argentine) mate and deposit their eggs. The larvae, called leptocephalous, hatch and begin their eastward migration. In 2 to 3 years they reach the typical snake-like form and are called elvers. At this point, the elvers group themselves in a mass near the mouths of rivers, then change color (yellow eels) and begin to swim upstream. Eels can even travel distances of dozens of feet on land, and they can live in just a few inches or centimetres of water.

Elephant-Trunk Fish: A freshwater fish of the family Mormyridae, found only in Africa. This fish has an elongated lower lip, which it uses to probe the mud of the bottom to find the small animals upon which it feeds.

Fin: A swimming appendage, typical of many aquatic animals such as fish and cetaceans (whales and dolphins).

ocean moonfish

Flying Fish: A group of fish of the family Exocoetidae, these fish do not really fly, as suggested by its name, rather, they glide in midair above the surface of the water to escape such predators as marine birds, large fish, and dolphins. Some species can travel up to 130 ft (40 m) in this manner.

Fry: Recently hatched, or very young, fish.

wrasse

Gills: The breathing organs of fish and many other aquatic animals as well as some mollusks. Gills have a slightly feathery appearance and are rich in blood vessels, which allow the absorption of oxygen from the water and the expulsion of carbon dioxide. In fish, gills are protected by a bony plate, or operculum, which also pumps water over the gills to continuously supply oxygen.

tilapia

Gilthead Sea Bream: This ocean fish of the family Sparidae takes its name from the gold stripe between its eyes. It can reach up to 28 in (70 cm) in length and lives in the coastal waters of the Mediterranean Sea, the Black Sea, and the eastern Atlantic Ocean.

Goldfish: This member of the family Cyprinidae is native to east Asia. In the wild, goldfish may grow to 17 in (45 cm) in length and weigh as much as 6.5 lbs (3 kg). Domestic goldfish rarely grow to more than 6 in (15 cm) in length.

Killifish: This bony fish belongs to the Cyprinid family. It is a very popular and hardy aquarium fish. In the wild it is found in the Americas, Africa, Asia, and in southern Europe. Killifish help to control the mosquito population by eating the insect's larvae.

Lionfish: A member of the family Scorpaenidae, it is found in the tropical waters of the Indian and the Pacific Oceans. The lionfish has a strong poison in the sharp spines of its fins and is a ferocious predator. The fins are divided into ribbon-like strips, with

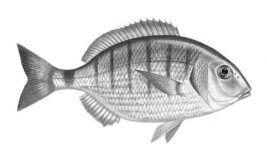

sea bream

elephant-trunk fish

Gray Mullet: A bony fish, member of the family Mugilidae, which lives in coastal sea waters less than 100 ft (30 m) deep, as well as in the brackish mouths of rivers. The gray mullet reproduces only in sea water where the female, courted by ten or more males, deposits up to 7,000,000 eggs on the ocean floor. Mullets live in schools, are very fast swimmers, and can jump several yards above the water's surface. These fish live on algae, crustaceans, worms, mollusks, and plant waste.

Grouper: A member of the Percidae and Serranidae families, the common grouper, found in the Mediterranean Sea and the eastern Atlantic Ocean, is up to 55 in (140 cm) long. It lives along rocky coastlines as well as on the ocean floor, and is found at depths of several hundred yards. Very old groupers are rather calm-natured, whereas the young are more restless. The grouper eats live prey, which it captures with a surprising burst of speed and swallows whole, sucked into its enormous mouth.

octopus

surmullett

those of the pectoral fins being longer than the fish's body. With its pectoral fins open, the lionfish pushes small fish into corners and captures them by sucking them into its mouth.

Lobster: This decapod (from the Greek, meaning ten-footed) crustacean belongs to the family Palinuris. Lobsters have long antennae and can grow as long as 18 in (45 cm) and weigh nearly 18 lbs (8 kg).

Longnose Gar: A member of the family Lepisosteidae found in North America from the Great Lakes to Florida, the longnose gar can grow to a length of over 71 in (180 cm) and weigh more than 70 pounds (32 kg). The female can live to the age of 22 and deposits about 27,000 eggs at a time, which then stick to vegetation in the water. The eggs hatch in 6 to 7 days and the young grow about 1 in (2.5 cm) per day.

Neon Tetra: A freshwater bony fish belonging to the family Characidae, these fish are very popular in aquariums. Originally from the Rio Putumayo in eastern Peru, they are now successfully bred in captivity. They live in large schools and take their name from their bright, metallic blue and red coloring that shines like a neon light sign.

Ocean Moonfish: This bony fish belongs to the family Molidae and is found in every sea in the world, taking its name from its disk-like shape. The ocean moonfish can grow to a length of nearly 10 ft (3 m) and weigh nearly 900 pounds (408 kg). It is probably the most fertile fish in the world. One female can produce up to 300 million eggs.

paradise fish

Parrotfish: A bony fish of the family Scaridae that is found in warm temperate seas and tropical waters all over the world. The parrotfish's name is derived from its flashy coloring and the "beak" formed by its teeth. With its beak, the parrotfish can crush and swallow great quantities of calcium-containing material from the coral reefs.

Piranha: This freshwater, bony fish of the family Characidae is known for its ferocious attacks on its victims, which it tears to pieces with sharp, triangular, razor-sharp teeth. The piranha is a gregarious fish that lives near the shoreline of the Amazon River and its tributaries. Piranhas care for their eggs and protect their young.

butterflyfish

Pufferfish: The name given to various species of the family Tetraodontidae. Pufferfish are found in tropical waters, but there are freshwater species as well. Like the porcupine fish, pufferfish, or puffers, can blow themselves up with water until they look like balls.

cuttlefish

Octopus: This cephalopod mollusk has eight prehensile, very flexible tentacles equipped with suckers that enable it to cling to rocks and to capture prey. This animal can change color quickly by contracting and expanding special pigment cells called chromatophores. To escape its enemies, the octopus discharges a black pigment, or ink, into the water, momentarily hiding it from view.

scorpion fish

Salmon: This bony fish of the family Salmonidae is represented by a large number of species in northern oceans and the rivers that flow into these waters. The salmon is anadromous, and travels from the ocean to rivers in order to spawn. During the migration, the appearance of some species changes dramatically, for example, pink salmon develop a humpback.

lionfish

Porcupine Fish: A bony fish belonging to the Diodontidae family, it is found in nearly all the warm seas on Earth. It has a round body, a small tail that is always moving, and a large head. Its eyes are very large and move independently from one another. The porcupine fish can use binocular vision. The quills that give this fish its name are very long and normally lie flat against its body. If this fish is disturbed, it inflates itself with water until it is a spine-covered ball. It eats small crustaceans and mollusks.

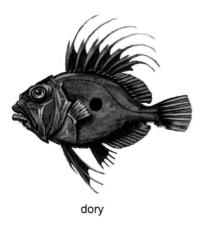

dory

Paradise Fish: A member of the family Anabantidae, this fish is found in east Asia in shallow water and rice paddies. It can survive for long periods breathing air from the atmosphere, thanks to an extra respiratory organ called a labyrinth. Unlike the young of this species, the adults cannot live together because they fight among themselves.

Protopterus: This freshwater, bony fish of the family Lepidosirenidae lives in the lakes and rivers of Africa. The protopterus, or lungfish, survives the dry season by burrowing into the mud and covering itself with mucus. Once the surrounding water has completely evaporated, this fish is able to breathe the atmospheric air with its lunglike air bladder.

Scalare: This freshwater, bony fish of the family Cichlidae is also known as an angelfish. It is a popular aquarium fish that grows to a length of 6 in (15 cm) and a height of 10 in (26 cm). It lives among dense vegetation and feeds on small water creatures. Parents care for their young.

pufferfish

Scales: Although the skin of fish can be bare, in most cases it is covered in scales—a dermal tissue that overlaps like shingles on a roof. Together with the layer of mucus secreted by glands located in the epidermis, the scales protect the skin.

Scorpion Fish: A marine, bony fish of the family Scorpaenidae with poison glands at the base of the dorsal fins and on the sides of the head. The large-scaled scorpion fish is non-migratory and solitary, preferring the rocky coastline of the western Atlantic Ocean and the Mediterranean Sea. It hides among the rocky crags, blending in to its surroundings despite its bright red coloring. It either pursues its prey or suddenly opens its large mouth causing a strong suction action that quickly draws the prey into its mouth.

Sea Anemone: Despite its resemblance to the flower from which it takes its name, the sea anemone is an animal belonging to the class Anthozoa, which includes about 7,000 species.

longnose gar

Most anthozoans are marine animals that live on the sea floor, and include coral. Sea anemones are often large and brightly colored with numerous stinging tentacles arranged in many concentric rows around their mouth. They immobilize their prey—small fish and crustaceans—with the poison in these tentacles.

Sea Bass: A bony fish of the family Serranidae, it can attain a length of 3 ft (1 m) and weigh up to 22 lbs (10 kg). This fish lives in small schools and migrates to the mouths of streams to spawn.

Sea Bream: This marine, bony fish of the family Sparidae is found in the Mediterranean Sea and eastern Atlantic Ocean, from France to Senegal.

trumpet fish and parrotfish

Living in the crevices of reefs to a depth of 100 ft (30 m), this fish feeds on animals that live among the submerged rocks. The sea bream grows to 15 in (40 cm) in length.

Sea Horse (Hippocampus): A group of bony fish of the Syngnathidae family having horse-like heads tilted downwards towards the stomach. The sea horse has a finless tail with which it can use to attach itself to marine vegetation. Males have an incubation pouch in which they keep the eggs and the larvae after they have hatched.

Sea Urchin: These members of the invertebrate family Echinodermata are related to starfish and holothurians

(sea cucumbers). The sea urchin is a bottom-dweller and uses its spines to move. It feeds on small animals, vegetation and detritus.

killifish

Shark: The name for a group of fish, some being enormous ocean predators, belonging to the family Isuridae. One notorious shark, the great white, can grow up to 23 ft (7 m) in length, and can weigh 33 tons. The great white shark is found in the Caribbean, and they can be voracious and have been known to attack humans.

Skate: A cartilaginous fish of the family Rajidae. This flat fish has a long tail with rudimentary electric organs on either side. The skate is oviparous, which means it produces eggs that develop and hatch outside the body. Its eggs are large and have a membranous shell. Most skates are saltwater animals, but there are a few freshwater species as well.

Snipefish: A group of bony fish in the family Macrorhamphosidae found worldwide, particularly in the tropics and subtropics. It is also called the trumpet fish because of its long snout.

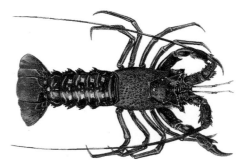

lobster

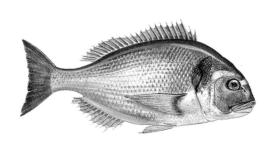

gilthead sea bream

Swordtail: This freshwater, bony fish belongs to the family Poecillidae and is a popular aquarium fish. In the wild, the swordtail lives in small schools and is found from Mexico to Guatemala. The swordtail is ovoviviparous, which means it gives birth to live fish after incubating the eggs in its body.

Tilapia: A freshwater, bony fish of the family Cichlidae, it originates in West Africa. The male uses its strong jaws to dig a spawning pit. After the eggs are fertilized, the female scoops them up

gray mullet

Surmullet: This marine, bony fish of the family Mullidae lives in the Mediterranean and the Black Seas, as well as the eastern Atlantic Ocean. The female, which grows to 15 in (40 cm) is larger than the male, which grows only to 12 in (30 cm). Unlike the red mullet, which lives only in sandy areas, the surmullet lives in both sandy and rocky areas. It reproduces in the summer near the coastline, where it deposits eggs that float due to their oily coating. In the autumn, it moves out to deeper waters.

Swordfish: This fish is the only species of the family Xiphiidae. The swordfish may grow to a length of 15 ft (4.5 m), weigh up to 1,100 lbs (500 kg), and can swim at speeds of 40 to 60 mph (60 to 100 km/h). It is distinguished by its long sword, formed by fusion of the jaw bones, which it uses to hunt for food and to defend itself against larger fish. The swordfish has neither scales nor teeth. It lives in the open waters of tropical and temperate seas throughout the world.

batfish

Wrasse: A bony marine fish of the family Labridae that is found in the Mediterranean Sea, the Black Sea and the eastern Atlantic Ocean. This fish lives near the coast in depths of up to nearly 400 ft (120 m). Its main characteristic is that, during its life, it not only changes its gender from female to male, but also its coloring. The wrasse can grow to a length of nearly 10 in (25 cm) and is raised in marine aquariums.

with her mouth where they remain until they hatch. This is known as oral incubation. Although the female continues to eat during incubation, she consumes less, losing considerable weight. When the young hatch, they remain in the mother's mouth until they can swim independently.

Weever: This bony marine fish of the family Trachinidae is widely found throughout the Mediterranean, in the eastern Atlantic and in the Baltic Sea. The spiny rays of the dorsal fin and the prickles on the gill covers are connected to glands that produce venom injected upon contact with a predator, or even humans. The venom destroys red blood cells and paralyzes the nerves, causing very sharp pain. This fish lives at the bottom of sandy waters and feeds on prawns and small fish, which it captures from its hiding place with lightning speed.

weever

porcupine fish

317

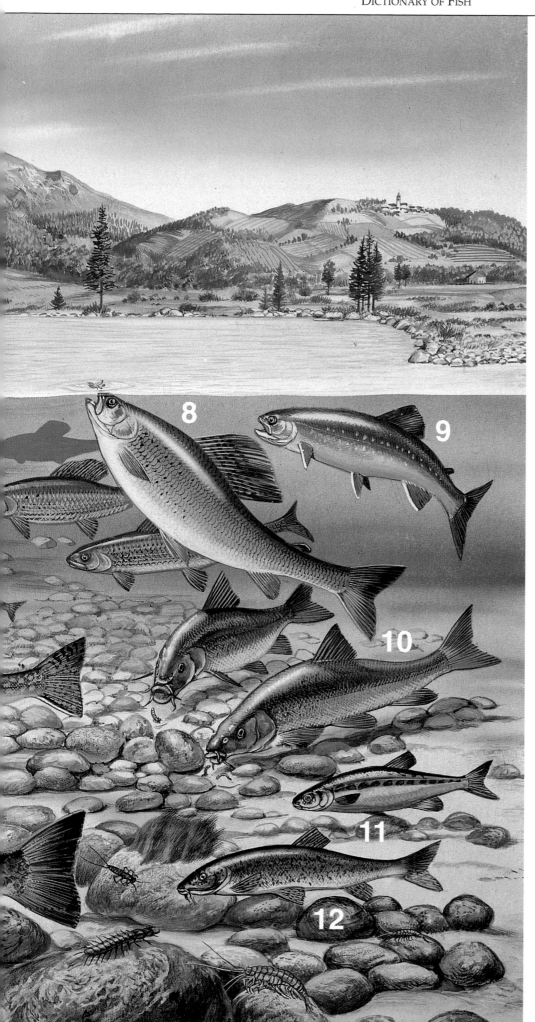

A RIVER'S ROUTE TO THE SEA

Stages of a River's Course

From its source to its mouth, a river can be divided into zones called stages, each having its own particular environment and fish population. At the source, or upper stage, live salmonid fish, a family that includes the trout. Further downriver, at the middle stage, the cyprinids, such as carp, are found. Finally, at the lower stage we typically find the sole and other soleids.

Near the river's source, or upper stage, the river is little more than a brook, flowing out of the mountains over a floor of large, smooth rocks and coarse gravel. The water is rich in oxygen and rather cold (41 to 59°F, or 5 to 15°C). This is the ideal environment for trout, char, and the grayling, all members of the family Salmonidae.

1. **European trout**
2. **rainbow trout**
3. **miller's thumb**
4. **brook trout**
5. ***marmorata* trout**
6. **crayfish**
7. **caddis fly worms**
8. **grayling**
9. **char**
10. **Italian barbel**
11. **minnow**
12. **Mediterranean barbel**

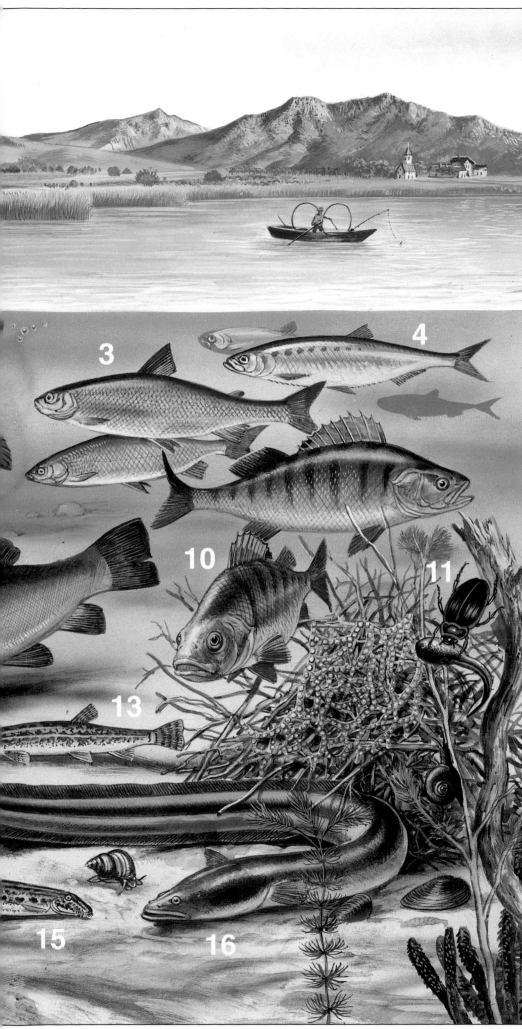

The Middle Stage

Here, the river has passed the rapids and waterfalls of its upper stage and now makes its way through the plains, found between the mountains and the sea. The river flows more slowly, the shores are covered with vegetation and, on the sand and gravel-covered bottom, there is a thick growth of aquatic plants. This is the beginning of the cyprinids' region.

The water of the middle stage is warmer (53 to 64°F, 12 to 18°C) than the upper stage, and it contains less oxygen than the salmonid's region. Cyprinid fish that live here have less demanding environmental needs than the salmonids. Their diet is made up of a large variety of animals and vegetation. Some cyprinids, like the tench, forage about in the silt on the river bottom.

1. bleak
2. zander
3. whitefish
4. twaite shad
5. rudd
6. freshwater blenny
7. Italian nase
8. dace
9. tench
10. perch
11. water beetle
12. chub
13. spined loach
14. stroemling
15. common loach
16. eel

The Meandering River

The middle stage of the river's course flows more slowly and has wide bends called meanders. The water is warm (60 to 68°F or 16 to 20°C), there is less oxygen, and fine sand covers the bottom. Along the course of the river, some of these meanders become closed off by sediment carried by the river, and crescent-shaped ponds are created.

The pike is a typical dweller of the middle stage of the river. Pike are slender fish that are very fast at capturing small fish. The pike's strong tail gives it the burst of speed it needs for lightning fast take-offs. This fish has an enormous mouth full of sharp teeth.

1. **Lake Garda carp**
2. **mosquitofish**
3. **mirror carp**
4. **green frog**
5. **carp**
6. **crucian carp**
7. **wild goldfish**
8. **largemouth bass**
9. **sunfish**
10. **gudgeon**
11. **pike**
12. **dace**
13. **burbot**
14. **leech**
15. **catfish**
16. **three-spined stickleback**
17. **river lamprey**

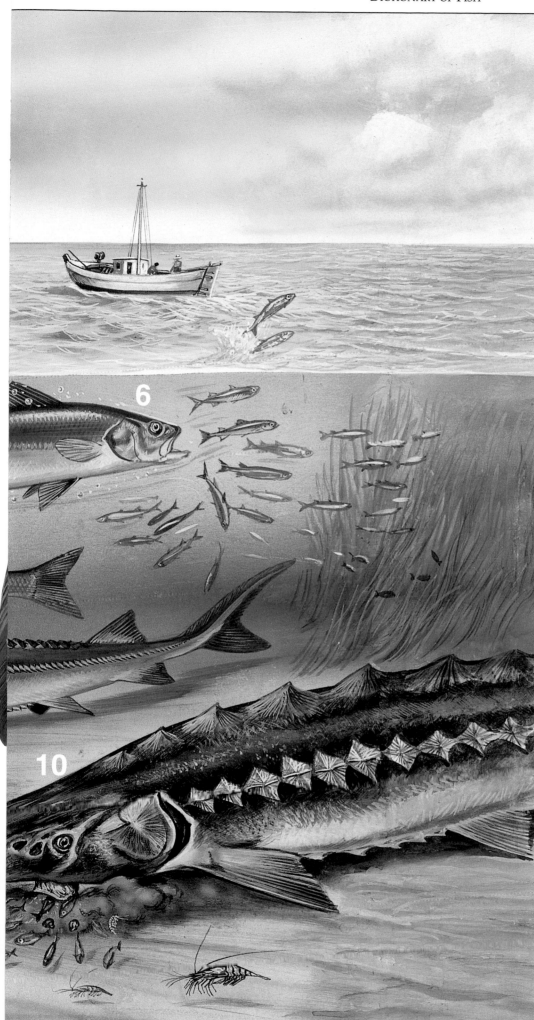

From Freshwater to Saltwater

Usually before the river flows into the ocean, it becomes quite wide. The river is slow-moving and the bottom is covered with a layer of silt that is rich in nutrients. As a result, there is a dense growth of reeds and aquatic vegetation. The freshwater mixes with saltwater and many species of fish living in this part of the river can also survive in the ocean.

Adaptability

Many fish that live at the mouth of the river, such as the gray mullet or the sea bass, are originally from the ocean. The ability to live in environments with such different concentrations of salt is a sign of fish that have adapted and evolved in ways that most fish have not.

1. **mallard duck**
2. **water striders**
3. **Alice shad**
4. **water snake**
5. **newt**
6. **sea bass**
7. **grass carp**
8. **gray mullet**
9. **great white sturgeon**
10. **common sturgeon**
11. **sheathfish**
12. **goby**
13. **mussel**
14. **tubificids**
15. **planarian**
16. **clam**

The hornbill has a funny horned helmet on its head and beak.

Bird: A warm-blooded, egg-laying vertebrate with forelimbs modified into wings that, in most species, are used for flying. Feathers cover the body. The shape of a bird's beak is generally adapted to the type of food eaten.

Black Vulture: This large bird of prey lives in Asia and Europe. Few remain in Europe because of humans and the scarcity of their food, which is usually dead animals.

Blackbird: The male blackbird is black with a yellow beak while the female is brown all over. They usually build their nest in low bushes and feed on insects. Generally timid, the blackbird becomes bolder when it lives in populated areas.

The three "thorns" around the araponga's beak are made of beak material, not feathers.

Bleeding-Heart Dove: Living in the forests of the Philippines, this dove's feathers are mostly gray except for a large patch of red feathers on its breast, which gives it its name.

Booby: Nesting on ocean islands, this bird spends most of the day skimming over the water in search of fish, which it captures by diving into the water.

Bunting: This bird lives in open fields bordered by hedges and bushes where it nests. The adult feeds primarily on seeds, but nesting young are mainly fed insects.

Buzzard: These birds of prey are found throughout the world. Buzzards hunt either by surveying the surrounding area from a high perch or by flying in search of its prey of small rodents,

In the spring, the sky is often full of swallows.

snakes, and insects.

Canary: A native of the Canary Islands west of Africa, this bird is now a domestic pet found all over the world because of its melodious song. Over the years, canaries have been bred to produce colorful plumage not found in the wild.

Cardinal: With its red plumage, crested head and black ring around its beak, it is a favorite songbird. The cardinal is found in wooded areas, where it finds the seeds and insects that make up its diet.

Cassowary: Weighing about 175 lb (80 kg), this large bird cannot fly. The large horned crest on its head helps the cassowary clear a path when running through thick vegetation.

Chaffinch: This finch was studied in depth by Charles Darwin, the father of the theory of evolution. The chaffinch lives in the Galapagos Islands and uses

Geese occasionally invade wheatfields to eat grain.

long thorns from a cactus to dig under the bark of trees as it looks for insect larvae to eat.

Chick: A term meaning the young of any bird, but particularly the offspring of the domestic chicken. Chicks are active from the moment they hatch. They follow their mother in search of food. At night they seek the warmth of her feathers.

The marabou eats the remains of animals killed and left by predators.

The hoopoe has a feather crest that it can open like a fan.

Common Magpie: Related to the crow, this black and white bird has blue-green wings and a long tail. The magpie is non-migratory, and prefers to remain in the same area all year. Many people consider the bird a thief because it is attracted to shiny objects, such as jewelry, which it will fly away with and hide.

Common Snipe: This long-legged bird builds its nest in dry areas of marshes. The snipe uses its long beak to find mollusks in the mud. During courtship, the snipe spreads two of its tail-feathers in flight so that the wind passing through them makes a particular sound.

The adult chaffinch eats seeds that have fallen to the ground.

Coot: This fairly common bird is not hard to find in swamps and marshes. Its feathers are dark, and its beak and forehead white. If frightened, the coot first gathers speed by running on the water before it takes flight.

Cordon Bleu: Common in Africa, this bird is much sought-after by bird lovers because of its brilliant plumage. The cordon bleu was raised by the bird keepers of King Louis XV of France.

Crane: This large migratory bird adapts well to captivity, but it is endangered in the wild because its wetland habitats are gradually disappearing. It is a protected bird throughout the world.

Crossbill: The end of this bird's beak is crossed. It is ideal for opening the pine cones of conifer trees, such as pine and spruce, to get at the seeds.

Crow: A crow's plumage can be all black, but also black and gray. It resembles the raven, though it is somewhat smaller. When in groups, one member will serve as a look-out and warns the others at the approach of danger.

The bleeding-heart dove is recognizable from other doves by the large red mark on its breast.

Cuckoo: This fairly large bird does not generally build a nest of its own, but lays its eggs in the nests of other birds. When it hatches, the young cuckoo tips the other eggs or young out of the nest. In this way, it remains the only one left to be fed by the unsuspecting adoptive parent, who soon finds itself smaller than the baby it is caring for.

Curlew: In damp areas where it lives, the curlew uses its long beak to find worms and mollusks in the mud. The male stands guard a few hundred feet from the nest. Like other birds, if it sees its nest threatened, it will pretend to be injured to draw predators away from the nest.

Dodo: This bird lived on the island of Mauritius, but has been extinct since 1680. The dodo was a flightless pigeon over 3 ft (1 m) long with a tufted tail. The Europeans that colonized the island brought pigs and monkeys that killed off the dodo. All

The Malaysian pheasant is one of the most colorful and decorative of birds.

that remains today of the dodo are a few drawings from the period, and some skeletons.

Down: The very light and delicate under feathers that birds have to maintain body heat rather than to fly. An excellent insulating material, down is used by humans to stuff blankets and line jackets.

Duck: A generic name that includes many species: the mallard, the pintail, wood ducks, the widgeon, the teal and garganey teal, the merganser, and many others. Ducks have been raised since ancient times for their meat.

The Chinese magpie's plumage is more colorful than that of the green magpie's.

The golden-breasted starling has multi-colored feathers unlike other starlings.

Hill Mynah: About the size of a pigeon, this bird is black, and has a yellow beak and yellow wattles beneath its eyes. It is a very good mimic of the human voice, as well as other sounds.

Hoatzin: Living in the dense forests of South America, the hoatzin spends most of its time perching. Local inhabitants call it the "stinking bird" due to its unpleasant odor.

The rhinoceros hornbill lives on fruit that it throws in the air and catches in flight.

Hoopoe: A very striking bird, the hoopoe has a cinnamon-colored body and crested head, and white and black bars on its wings. It hunts on land, eating insects, worms and spiders.

Hornbill: Over its strong beak, this unusual-looking bird has a very light, bony 'helmet.' The hornbill flies slowly from tree to tree in search of the fruit on which it lives.

Hummingbird: These tiny, beautiful birds are only found in the Americas. By beating their wings up to eighty times per second, hummingbirds can hover in the air to suck nectar out of flowers with their long beak. They are so lightweight that they can attach their tiny nest to the branches of trees with threads from spider webs.

Jackdaw: These birds are similar to crows but smaller. Jackdaws build their nests close to those of pigeons in order to eat the eggs and the young left unattended.

Kestrel: This small, very common falcon preys on small mammals and insects.

The fieldfare, a type of thrush, lives in the woods, but often goes to human settlements in search of food.

It will soar 65 to 100 ft (20 to 30 m) in the air, and then hovers like a helicopter while scanning the terrain for prey.

King Penguin: This penguin is the second-largest, next to the emperor penguin. As with all penguins, it lives in the Antarctic. Its young are brown whereas the adults are gray-black and white, with a yellow-orange neck and cheeks.

Kingfisher: Much time is spent by this bird perched in a tree above either fresh or salt water. When a small fish swims by, the kingfisher dives into the water and catches it with its long, sharp beak. Its nests are found in tunnels dug into embankments.

Kite: Found only in the "Old World" (Europe, Africa and Asia), this bird eats both land and aquatic animals. Where there is an abundance of food, it establishes large colonies. In the autumn, European kites migrate to Africa.

The pelican's beak includes a large pouch to store its catch.

Kiwi: This bird has just two short stumps for wings and cannot fly. It is a nocturnal hunter and feeds on insects and other small invertebrates. The kiwi is native to New Zealand and is also its national emblem.

Lady Amherst Pheasant: This is one of the most colorful pheasants, and has one of the longest tails, making it a very popular bird for ornamental gardens. In the wild, it can be found in China, in the thick bamboo forests where it feeds upon new shoots.

Lark: The song of the lark varies a great deal, depending on the occasion. It builds its nest on the ground in places chosen by the male, who arrives about a month before the female. It eats seeds and insects that it finds in fields.

Little Owl: This attractive, nocturnal bird of prey has big, yellow eyes. Unfortunately, the little owl has been the victim of an absurd belief that it brings bad luck. Hunters, as well, have blamed the little owl for preying on the birds and other small animals that they are in search of.

The scarlet ibis of South America searches for its food in shallow water.

The scarlet macaw and the blue-and-yellow macaw differ in their coloring.

Little Winged Plover: This wading bird lives along fresh and saltwater shores. If a predator threatens to come near its nestlings, this bird pretends to be injured and attracts the enemy's attention. At the last moment, it will fly off, fooling the intruder.

Macaw: This large, brightly colored South American parrot uses its claws both to climb in trees, and to bring food to its beak to eat. The scarlet macaw's feathers are mostly red, while the blue-and-yellow macaw is yellow with blue head and wings.

Beware of the magpie: it has been know to steal coins, rings and other shiny objects.

Mallard: Considered the most common duck, the plumage of the male and female mallard are quite different. The female is brown all over, whereas the male has a bright green head, a white ring around its neck, a brick red breast and body, and wings that are gray, white, and black. This duck is raised for its meat. It is also a common addition to the ponds of zoos and parks.

Marabou: Found throughout Africa, the marabou stork eats nearly anything edible including animal carcasses.

Migration: This is the mass movement of birds, or other animals, from one region to another. Many birds, such as swallows, geese and storks, spend winters in warmer regions and summers in cooler regions.

Moorhen: Easy to spot in lakes and marshes where it lives, the moorhen is dark with a few white bars, red eyes, and a red and yellow bill. To escape predators, it prefers to go underwater, rather than fly.

Nightingale: Renowned for its song, and not its plain brown appearance, the nightingale is heard by day as well as by night. The song can be quite

The goshawk is a medium-sized bird of prey that feeds on small mammals and reptiles.

varied and is distinguished by pure, clear notes that can be heard far away.

Northern Oriole: Living in most North American habitats, this skillful weaver builds a very distinctive and complex nest by weaving strands of grass into a sack, which is attached to the branch of a tree.

Oropendola: A native of South America, the oropendola struts rather than hops. It feeds insects to its young. The adult, however, generally eats only seeds.

Osprey: This raptor (bird of prey) is dark on the upper part of its body and white on the lower part. The osprey can be found near salt water and fresh water. It eats only fish. At one time, the osprey was very common along the shores of the Mediterranean, but now there are few remaining.

The jacana looks for food while walking on floating lily pads.

Ostrich: This well-known, large and flightless African bird can outrun its predators most of the time. At one time, people used its feathers as fashion accessories. Today, the ostrich is raised for its meat. The belief that it hides its head in the sand when frightened is unfounded.

Owl: This nocturnal bird of prey flies without making a sound. The owl is traditionally considered the symbol of wisdom owing to its serious air and intelligent expression. In the past, it was widely believed that this bird had evil powers.

Parrots: These birds are found throughout the southern hemisphere. They have a short, powerful beak and vivid coloring. Members of this order include the macaw of South America, the cockatoo of Australia and New

When the little robin flies south, winter is on its way.

Zealand, which sports an upright tuft on its head, and the African parakeet, often captured for domestic aviaries. Parrots feed on seeds, fruit, and occasionally, on insects.

Pheasant: These game birds are raised in large numbers on reserves. In the wild, the males and females spend the winter in separate groups. In the spring, the males look for a place to build their nest. Pheasants build their nests on the ground.

Pied Flycatcher: This bird waits in the branches of trees and expertly catches insects as they fly by.

Pied Wagtail: A very graceful bird with a slender black and white body, the pied wagtail builds its nest near the water, but can adapt to living anywhere.

Pigeon: A name used to indicate certain birds that differ only in their size or plumage. This family includes the dove, the turtle-dove, the wood pigeon, and the common pigeon. They are found all over the world

The griffon vulture is a large vulture living in Europe and Asia.

The beak of the hawfinch is strong enough to crack olive and cherry pits.

Partridge: This wild fowl is related to the chicken, and it generally stays on the ground where it searches for seeds, leaves, and young shoots. It likes to roll around in sand and gravel.

Peacock: Known for its magnificent tail, this native of India and Sri Lanka has been raised throughout the world since ancient times. It is still prized in many public and private gardens. In Ancient Rome they were also raised for food. The peacock is the male peafowl.

Pelican: These birds hunt in groups. Swimming side by side, they direct frightened fish towards shallow water where they are easier to capture. Their long beaks have pouches that can hold many fish. Pelicans can then take a full pouch of food back to their nests.

The dodo bird of the island of Mauritius was the size of a turkey. It became extinct three hundred years ago.

Peregrine Falcon: This bird of prey can attain speeds of over 200 mph (350 km/h) when it plunges to capture a bird in flight. Since ancient times, this bird has been domesticated and trained to hunt in cooperation with humans, an art known as falconry.

The collared dove is found in aviaries throughout the world.

with the exception of the poles. Some are raised so that they will always return to their nests when they are taken far from home. These are carrier or homing pigeons, and have been used for centuries to carry messages attached to their legs.

Ptarmigan: This bird changes color during the year. In winter, it is white with a black tail, and in summer it is a mottled brown color. The ptarmigan builds its nest on the ground. The male will act as a decoy to lure intruders or predators away from the nest.

Puffin: This marine bird of unusual appearance lives along the coasts of northern oceans. Its plumage is white and black, and its short, thick beak has vivid colours ranging from red

to yellow to blue. When it catches fish, it keeps some in its mouth to eat later in its nest and to feed to its young.

Quetzal: Found in Central America, this bright red and green bird has a short beak and looks like a parrot. The young are fed insects and other small animals, but the adults eat only fruit. The quetzal is the national emblem of Guatemala, whose currency is also named after this bird.

Raptor: All birds of prey were formerly classified as raptors. Now they are divided into two orders: the diurnal Falconiformes and the nocturnal Strigiformes.

Redstart: This small songbird has a red tail and is related to the sparrow. When the redstart leaves its nest for a moment, a cuckoo will often come and lay an egg in it. The baby cuckoo quickly grows to be larger than the redstart, which has to work very hard to feed it.

The bateleur eagle performs amazing aerial acrobatics.

Rhea: Like the ostrich, which it resembles, the rhea is unable to fly. A native of South America, it congregates in large flocks and eats any type of food, from vegetation to small animals.

In Canada and the United States, a roasted turkey is part of the traditional Christmas dinner.

Rhinoceros Hornbill: This Asian hornbill has black and white feathers with a yellowish beak and neck. Like other hornbills, it has an impressive bony "helmet" between the top of its head and its beak. The rhinoceros

The nightingale is quite ordinary in appearance, but has a varied and melodious song.

hornbill builds its nest inside a tree and makes the opening so small that the female cannot leave during the nesting period. The male feeds her through the opening in the tree.

Roadrunner: A fast-moving North American bird that lives in deserts, the roadrunner prefers to run rather than fly. Its feet have two toes pointing forward and two backwards, so its tracks are easily identified. The roadrunner eats insects, reptiles, and even poisonous snakes.

Robin: Found throughout Europe and North America, robins build their nests in low bushes and are ground feeders. A sociable bird, the robin will let people approach, but staunchly defends its territory from other robins.

Rook: A large, iridescent, black bird, the rook is found nearly everywhere in the world, in many different environments. This bird will eat almost anything, although it prefers meat. For this reason, it preys upon other birds, taking their eggs and young.

The blackbird is no stranger to life in large cities. The male has shiny black feathers and a yellow beak.

Rooster: The male of the domestic fowl, usually the chicken, which is raised throughout the world for meat and eggs. The female is less colorful than the male, and has a crest and wattles that are smaller. In the henhouse, the rooster has little tolerance for other males and will engage in vicious fights with potential rivals.

Scarlet Ibis: Completely red from beak to tail feather, the ibis lives near waterways and feeds on small animals. In Ancient Egypt, the sacred ibis, a white species, was considered an incarnation of the god Thoth.

Sea Eagle: Now nearly extinct because of humans, the sea eagle builds its nest on rocky spurs or in trees near the sea. The sea eagle eats fish, skimming the water's surface and seizing its prey in its claws. It also eats land animals.

These gray cranes migrate by day and often by night, flying in a V formation or in a long line. They commonly fly at speeds of 30 mph (50 km/h).

Secretary Bird: This is a different sort of bird of prey from Africa. It has very long legs and, although able to fly very high, it hunts on the ground, killing its prey with its strong talons.

Shrike: This bird has an unusual habit. After capturing small prey such as frogs, mice, and lizards, the shrike spears them on a dry twig or long thorn to eat them later!

Skua: This bird lives in polar coastal regions. Very aggressive, it robs the nests of other birds, eating the eggs and young. It also attacks other birds flying with fish in their beaks and forces them to drop their prey, which the skua then seizes in midair.

Canaries are raised for their melodious song.

The snow bunting lives in the tundra, nesting on the rocky terrain.

Sparrow: This small bird has adapted to living in close proximity to humans around the world. In the evening at certain times of the year, some sparrows gather on the same tree and chirp noisily.

Starling: In autumn, these birds gather in large flocks. Moving in unison, they seem to form a dark cloud in the sky. At dusk, they gather in a tree, where they spend the night.

Steppes Eagle: Found on the steppes and semi-arid areas of Asia, this bird prefers to spend its time on the ground rather than flying. The adult is dark brown while the young are much lighter.

Canaries may vary in color from yellow to pink and orange to green.

Stork: This large white bird migrates long distances, at altitudes of up to nearly 3 miles (4,500 m). The stork builds its nest in very high places, such as towers, steeples, chimneys, trees, and telephone poles. It usually returns to the same nest every year. The stork is mute and communicates by snapping its beak.

Swallow: There are many species of swallows and all of them migrate. The common swallow often lives in populated areas where it will build a nest of mud and grass. Swallows eat insects that they catch in flight with their triangular beaks.

Swan: Large and graceful, the swan's plumage can be white or black. Clumsy on land, this bird prefers to swim rather than walk. The swan is frequently kept in ponds in city parks because of its majestic appearance on the water.

The white-breasted kingfisher feeds on fish, insects, and tadpoles.

Swift: Considered by some as the perfect flying machine, the swift spends most of its life in flight. Some species even sleep while flying! If it must land for any reason, the swift has difficulty taking off again. It flies at about 55 mph (90 km/h), but can attain speeds of up to 125 mph (200 km/h).

Sword-Billed Hummingbird: All hummingbirds have long beaks for sucking the nectar out of flowers. This hummingbird's beak is as long as its body!

Tawny Owl: This bird of prey hunts at night. During the day, the tawny owl dozes in the shade, where its color makes it very hard to see. Despite its harmless appearance, this owl quickly and aggressively attacks its prey.

Tern: This sea bird does not willingly venture away from the coast where it lives. A very skillful diver, the tern

The greenfinch lives in woods and bushes.

searches for its food while flying, then folds its wings and dives into the water to skewer its prey with its pointed beak.

Thrush: Although small, this bird has great endurance and adaptability. It is able to live in many environments. The thrush feeds mainly on insects, but it is especially fond of snails. In winter, it eats a vegetarian diet due to the scarcity of its preferred food.

Tit: There are many species of these little birds. Tits are often found in gardens, especially when artificial nests are put out for them. In the summer, they eat insects and small animals. During the winter, they eat grubs.

Toucan: This tropical bird has an enormous beak and very colorful plumage. It prefers to remain perched in the trees and rarely comes down to the ground. The toucan eats the fruit it gathers by tossing it into the air and then catching and swallowing it.

The Japanese nightingale has a red beak and multi-colored plumage.

The cordon bleu is highly prized by bird lovers for its showy plumage.

Warbler: These common, charming birds are known for their persistent singing. Warblers constantly explore trees and bushes for insects, which it often catches in flight. It builds a round nest with a small opening.

Wattles: These ornamental, fleshy outgrowths are found on the head or neck of certain birds. Wattles are usually much more noticeable on males than on females.

Wood Grouse: This wildfowl lives primarily in deciduous forests, eating buds as well as rhododendrons and blueberries. The wood grouse is a popular game bird.

The toucan's beak is huge but very light.

Tree-Creeper: This bird is easily mistaken for a woodpecker because of its habit of climbing on tree trunks in search of larvae and insects that hide in the cracks of the bark. Unlike woodpeckers, though, the tree-creeper has a long, curved beak, and its plumage is less striking.

Turkey: Native to North America, and now found throughout the world, this bird is raised for its excellent meat. The male has a large red wattle on its neck.

The Baltimore oriole weaves grasses and even cloth and string into its nest.

Woodpecker: Usually sighted clinging onto tree trunks, woodpeckers make holes in trees with their beaks as they search for insects hiding in the bark. Even its nest, which it keeps very clean, is a hole in a tree trunk.

Wren: This very small, drab bird has a song that is very loud and can be heard from quite a distance.

The flycatcher snatches insects in midair.

Turtledove: This relative of the pigeon has a slim body and graceful appearance. It is very aggressive towards birds of its own species when protecting its territory, even to the point of killing potential rivals.

Wallcreeper: This gray bird has red wings with black bands. Living in the high mountains, the wallcreeper climbs among the rocks and uses its long beak to explore crevices for insects.

Woodcock: Found in the forests, the woodcock blends well with the leaves in the trees. Unfortunately for the woodcock, it is one of the birds most sought-after by hunters. The woodcock builds its nest on the ground. If threatened while sitting on her eggs, the female will not move until the very last moment.

Wild geese can fly very well. The domestic goose is often raised with chickens and turkeys.

DICTIONARY OF REPTILES AND AMPHIBIANS

REPTILES

Aesculapian Snake: This common European snake prefers to live in trees or on stone walls in fields. It loves to lie in the sun to stay warm and it eats mice and rats. It is not poisonous.

Alligator Snapping Turtle: Found in the southern United States, this is the largest of the freshwater turtles. It usually hunts while submerged in a river, where it snaps up passing fish.

American Alligator: These large reptiles can reach a length of nearly 20 ft (6 m). The alligator lives in the southeastern United States where they are also bred in captivity.

In India, snake charmers use the deadly cobra in their performances, but, to be on the safe side, they remove the snake's fangs.

Anaconda: The largest snake in the world, the anaconda can reach a length of nearly 40 ft (11.4 m). It lives in South America near the water and feeds on animals that it strangles with its coils.

Basilisk: This slender lizard is such a fast runner that it can actually run on water. The basilisk lives in Central America.

The tortoise can hide its head, feet, and tail inside its shell.

Black Caiman: Similar to the crocodile, the black caiman lives near the Amazon River. While there were many black caimans at one time, they are now nearly extinct because of over-hunting.

Black Mamba: Like the cobra, this large snake can grow to over 13 ft (4 m) in length. The black mamba does not attack humans, but if threatened, will bite with extreme speed. Its poison is deadly.

Blind-Worm, or Slow Worm: Though it looks like a snake because it has no legs, the blind-worm is actually a small, completely harmless European lizard. It lives among roots or under rocks, and comes out to eat earthworms or insects.

Boa Constrictor: This large, non-poisonous snake lives in tropical and subtropical South and Central America. Like the python and the anaconda, it slowly crushes and suffocates its prey, which it then swallows whole, head first.

Chameleon: This lizard can change its skin color to blend in with its environment. Its eyes can look in different directions at the same time.

Coral snake: This brightly colored, red, yellow, and black snake is very poisonous.

Crocodiles: Some species of these lizards are small, measuring under 5 ft (1.5 m) in length. Others, such as the saltwater crocodile, can reach lengths of over 23 ft (7 m). Crocodiles are covered with very thick skin and armored scales.

Diced Water Snake: This snake can easily be raised in a terrarium. It will reproduce in captivity and can live to 15 years of age.

Dwarf Crocodile: The smallest of all crocodiles, the dwarf crocodile does not even reach 6 ft (2 m) in length. It lives in Africa in the wet, tropical forests. It is not aggressive towards humans.

The coral snake has a deadly bite. The harmless milk snake mimics the coral snake's colorings to frighten away enemies.

The female crocodile lays her eggs in nests in the sand, which is then warmed by the sun.

The male green lizard becomes very brightly colored during mating season.

Egg-Eating Snake: As its name suggests, this snake's diet consists of eggs, which it swallows whole. Even if the egg is quite large, the snake can swallow it by opening its mouth very wide.

European Pond Turtle: Weighing up to 2 lb (1 kg), this turtle nests near riverbanks, where it will dig a hole in which to hibernate for the winter.

European Viper, or Adder: This venomous snake has a stout body, a triangular head, and eyes that have a black vertical slit for pupils. It avoids humans, but will bite if disturbed or stepped on.

European Water Snake, or Grass Snake: This very common water snake has a bite that is harmless to humans.

The dabb lizard is a type of spiny-tailed agama that lives in burrows.

To protect itself against attack, this snake gives off a foul-smelling liquid.

Flying Dragon: This lizard lives in trees where it eats ants. It has folds of skin, called patagium, which form wings. When opened, these wings allow the animal to glide through the air for short distances.

Flying Snake: This snake is named for its ability to "glide" from one tree to another by holding its body straight and rigid.

Frilled Lizard: When threatened, this Australian lizard flares its wide collar and opens its mouth in an attempt to frighten off its attacker.

Galapagos Giant Tortoise: This giant tortoise can grow to more than 3 ft (1 m) in length. At one time hunted to the point of extinction, the Galapagos giant tortoise is now a carefully protected species.

Ganges Gavial: While there were once large populations of the Ganges gavial at one time, this species of crocodile is now nearly extinct because of hunting by poachers.

Garter Snake: Found in grasslands, marshes, and woodlands thoughout North America, the harmless garter snake is usually less than 24 in (60 cm) long. It feeds on insects, earthworms, and amphibians.

The egg-eating snake can swallow eggs much larger than itself.

Gecko: Found in all hot and temperate zones on Earth, this lizard is useful for humans because it feeds on the insects that often infest houses.

Green Lizard: This lizard is found in the fields of southern Europe. It is emerald green in color. The male's throat becomes turquoise during mating season.

The python is not poisonous. It kills its prey by crushing it.

Green Turtle: One of the most well-known turtles, the green turtle grazes on sea grasses. Most other species are carnivorous.

The snake-neck tortoise pulls its head into its shell by folding its neck into an S-shape.

Green Vine Snake : Green and very slender, this snake looks just like a jungle vine. Its venom is strong, but not strong enough to kill a human.

Hermann's Tortoise: This tortoise grows to 12 in (30 cm) in length and has a very thick, rounded shell.

Hooded Cobra: Probably the best known of the cobras, the hooded cobra lives in southern Asia, usually near water. Because its poison is so deadly,

The saltwater crocodile can grow to 20 ft (6 m) in length.

its fangs are removed if the cobra is used in performances with snake charmers.

Horned Asp: This snake lives in the sandy regions of North Africa. It moves sideways, leaving a distinctive track.

Horned Lizard: This member of the iguana family lives in North American deserts. Its body is covered with thorny scales. When threatened, this animal burrows into the sand at lightning speed to hide. Some horned lizards will even squirt a stream of blood from its eyes to frighten away attackers.

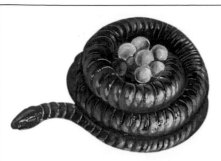

This ceacilian snake protects its newly laid eggs.

Iguana: This type of lizard is found mainly in Central America, where it is considered a delicacy. Some iguanas can grow to over 6 ft (2 m) in length.

Jackson's Chameleon: This African chameleon is easily recognized by the three long, forward-pointing horns on its face.

The frilled lizard opens its collar to frighten its enemies.

Komodo Dragon: Growing up to 10 ft (3 m) in length, this is the largest of all lizards. The Komodo dragon feeds on medium-sized mammals. It will attack humans only when provoked.

Leatherback Turtle: This marine turtle is huge, weighing up to 1,800 lb (800 kg). It lives in all three oceans and migrates long distances to lay its eggs in the sand of a specific beach.

Loggerhead Sea Turtle: This marine turtle can be seen swimming in the Mediterranean or other waters where it lives. The loggerhead was hunted for many decades. Now it is protected everywhere.

Marine Iguana: This iguana lives only on the Galapagos Islands. It is the only plant-eating lizard, and the only one that spends much of the time feeding in the sea. If threatened by its natural enemy the shark, the marine iguana will swim rapidly towards shore.

Matamata: A monstrous-looking South American tortoise, the matamata lives in fresh water. When a small fish swims by, it opens its jaws and sucks the fish into its mouth.

Nile Crocodile: This crocodile moves awkwardly on land, but swims with great agility. The Nile crocodile can grow up to 16 ft (5 m) in length.

At night, the gecko stays near lights, which attract the insects it feeds on.

Nile Monitor: This lizard can remain under water for up to one hour. The Nile monitor lays its eggs in termite nests to protect them from predators.

Python: This very large snake is found in the tropical regions of Africa and Asia. The python can reach over 25 ft (8 m) in length. The python is not poisonous. It wraps itself around its prey, crushing it, and then swallows it whole.

Rattlesnake: This snake has hard, interlocking scales at the end of its tail. When it is bothered or in danger, the snake shakes its tail, giving off a loud, scary, buzzing sound.

Reptiles: Cold-blooded, vertebrate animals whose bodies are covered with scales. The young emerge from eggs. In some reptiles, the eggs are hatched

The venom of the gaboon viper attacks the blood and central nervous system of its victim.

The Ganges gavial closely resembles a crocodile.

inside the mother and the young are born alive.

Saurian: This suborder includes many families of scaly reptiles, such as lizards, monitor lizards, geckos, iguanas, chameleons, and blind-worms. Saurians are found all over the world.

Scales: The scales of reptiles are thick layers of hardened skin that often overlap each other. The number of scales and the patterns they form help distinguish various species of reptiles.

Sea Snake: This marine snake lives in tropical seas, usually near coral reefs. It seldom attacks humans, but its bite is fatal.

Although it looks dangerous, the thorny devil is quite harmless.

Smooth Snake: A non-poisonous snake, the smooth snake prefers lizards to all other food, but will eat other prey, including poisonous snakes.

Snakes: Legless reptiles that slither along the ground. Some snakes inject poison into their enemies with special teeth. Others kill their prey by crushing it in their coils.

Snapping Turtle: This North American turtle lives in fresh water and eats a wide variety of aquatic plants and animals.

The monitor is a voracious animal that eats live prey.

The snapping turtle cannot retreat completely into its shell. For this reason, it relies on its powerful jaws to defend itself.

Sonda Gavial: This crocodile has a very long, thin snout. During the day, it warms itself in the sun; at night it hunts for fish.

Taipan: Growing to 11 ft (3 m) in length, the taipan is one of the deadliest snakes. Its venom affects the respiratory and blood systems, causing death in just a few seconds.

Tarente: This reptile looks like a gecko and has remained unchanged for 200 million years. It is found in the Mediterranean basin.

The basilisk moves so quickly that it can even run across water.

Tegu: This South American lizard is a vicious predator that wreaks havoc in henhouses, eating both eggs and chicks.

Thorny Devil: A lizard living in the deserts of Australia. Its body is completely covered with long quills. The thorny devil does not need to drink because it absorbs moisture from the air through its skin.

Trionychid: An aggressive freshwater turtle, the trionychid will vigorously defend itself against predators. The bump on its head looks like a long nose.

Viper: This snake likes sunny places. Most vipers give birth to live young.

Viperine Snake: This harmless grass snake has the same colorings as the common viper, a very dangerous snake. This coloring frightens many of its enemies.

Viviparous Lizard: This lizard lives in areas of lush tropical vegetation. The word viviparous means that the eggs hatch inside the mother's body so that she gives birth to live young.

The anaconda, the largest snake in the world, can swallow goat-size animals whole.

Wall Lizard: This lizard is very common in Europe. It stays on walls for long periods of time, basking in the sun. If attacked, this lizard breaks off a part of its tail, distracting its enemy.

Western Diamondback Rattlesnake: This large, colorful rattlesnake is found in North America, and it will attack when it is threatened.

The head of this plated lizard, or gerrhosaurine, is covered in rough plates.

AMPHIBIANS

The strawberry poison frog is small with red and black skin.

Amphibians: This group of vertebrate animals hatch from eggs in water and use gills to breathe. When they mature into adults, they live on land and use lungs to breathe. This change in form is known as metamorphosis.

Anura: This order of amphibians includes frogs, toads, and tree frogs. Their appearance changes dramatically from the larval to the adult stage. Adults do not have a tail and they grow legs. Their stocky and powerful back legs are designed for jumping.

Fire Salamander: Very common in hilly areas of Europe, this amphibian's skin produces a secretion that irritates the eyes and mucous membranes of predators.

The crested newt prefers to spend most of its time in water.

Fire-bellied toad: This toad of central and eastern Europe has a red or orange patch marbled with black on its underparts.

Frog: These amphibians have back legs that are designed to leap long distances. Frogs feed on insects, which they capture in midair with a flick of their sticky tongue. Their croaking sound is amplified by a pouch in its throat that puffs up and acts as a soundbox.

Gills: These organs are adapted for absorbing the oxygen from water. Fish and the larvae of amphibians use gills to breathe.

The dwarf siren has front legs only and moves like a snake.

Green Toad: This common European species is gray with large green markings.

Japanese Giant Salamander: Growing as long as 5 ft (1.5 m) and weighing up to 55 lb (25 kg), this shiny black salamander prefers to live in high mountain streams, where the water is clean and pure.

Malaysian Flying Frog: This small tree frog is able to "fly" from one branch to the next by spreading its heavily webbed feet.

Newt: There are many species of this amphibian. Most males have vivid coloring and some species have a large dorsal crest.

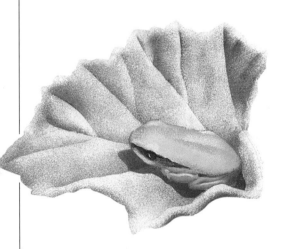

The tree frog lives in trees near pools of water. It can change color to blend in with its surroundings.

Olm: This salamander-like creature has rudimentary eyes that are covered with skin as well as very small legs. Unlike most amphibians, the olm has gills even as an adult. The olm lives in underground bodies of water.

Olympic Salamander: One of the smallest salamanders, the olympic salamander grows to no more than 4 in (10 cm) in length. It travels on open ground only during the mating season.

Slimy Salamander: Growing up to 8 in (20 cm) in length, this black salamander is very common in the United States. It lives in woods and feeds on worms, snails, and insects.

Strawberry Poison Frog: This beautiful red tree frog is one of 170 poison dart frogs found in Central and South America. Native people use the poison taken from the frog's skin to tip their hunting darts. The female strawberry poison frog carries each newborn tadpole on her back to the top of the forest canopy where she

The Asian horned toad looks like the leaves in which it hides.

deposits it in a pool of water that she finds on a leaf. Here the larva continues to develop.

Surinam Toad: The female of this South American species incubates its eggs in small pouches on its back. Offspring emerge after three months looking just like their parents.

Texas Blind Salamander: This salamander has thin, weak legs, and is believed to be blind because its eyes are covered with skin. The Texas blind salamander lives in the dark in underground bodies of water and feeds on small aquatic crustaceans.

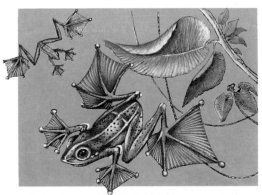

The webbing between the long toes and fingers of Malaysian flying frog allows it to glide briefly through the air from branch to branch.

Some salamanders secrete a mild poison to protect themselves from predators.

Tiger Salamander: When the weather or other conditions are unfavorable, this amphibian does not complete its metamorphosis and, even as an adult, keeps the form and habits of the aquatic larva stage.

Toad: This nocturnal amphibian is useful because it feeds on insect pests. When disturbed, it secretes a slightly irritating liquid.

The bullfrog is named for its size and harsh, loud call.

Tree Frog: These small, usually bright green frogs hide on the branches of trees, concealed by the leaves. The tree frog has sticky pads on the tips of its fingers and toes, enabling it to climb even on glass.

Two-Toed Amphiuma: As it swims, this long, slender amphibian closely resembles an eel. Its legs are very small and its feet have only two toes.

Urodela: This order of amphibians includes salamanders and newts. As adults, they retain characteristics adapted for swimming, such as a fin-like tail and a long body.

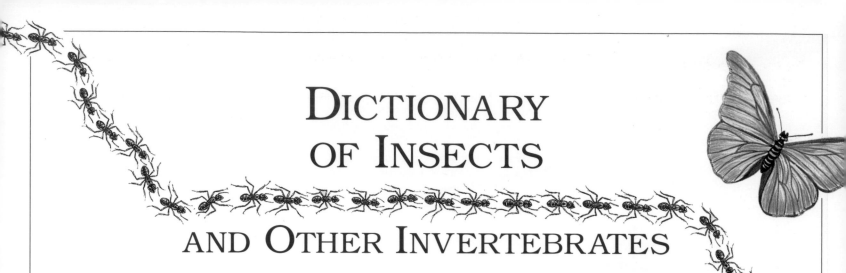

DICTIONARY OF INSECTS
AND OTHER INVERTEBRATES

Annelids: The group of worm-like invertebrates that includes earthworms, leeches, and other segmented worms. The bodies of these worm-like creatures are divided into identical rings, or segments, called metameres.

Ant: Also described as an "aculeated hymenopteran," which is an insect that stings or bites and is related to wasps and bees. The ant lives in large colonies, where each individual has a specific job: soldiers look after defending the colony; workers gather food and take care of the larvae; males, which generally have wings, take care of reproduction; and finally the queen, who cannot move very much due to her bulky size, is responsible for laying all the eggs.

The comma, or polygonia butterfly has a white C-shaped mark on its wings.

Antennae: The sensory organs many insects and arthropods have on their heads. They are used to explore the surrounding world.

Ant Lion: The adult ant lion resembles the dragonfly. The larva digs a cone-shaped hole in the ground and hides in it. If any prey falls into this hole, the ant lion traps it and eats it.

Apatura Iris: This large, showy European butterfly has wings that are black and iridescent purple with white stripes and spots. The rear wings have two red marks trimmed in black.

Aphid: Generally under ¼ inch (.5 cm) in length, with or without wings, aphids suck the sap out of green plants and leaves. Too many aphids on a single plant can kill it. Certain ants eat the sweet droplets that aphids secrete.

Arachnids: A class of primarily land-dwelling arthropods that includes spiders, scorpions, fleas, and mites. They have eight legs and no antennae.

The earwig spends the winter in a hole it has dug in the ground.

Bee: This insect is raised the world over for its products: wax, honey, royal jelly, and a type of glue called propolis. Bees live in large colonies. The queen is the only fertile female. During mating, she flies higher and higher so that only the strongest male can reach her. When a bee stings, it cannot remove its barbed stinger from the victim. The stinger, as well as the venom, become torn from the bee, causing it to die.

The golden beetle was considered sacred by both the Mayans and Egyptians.

The hummingbird hawkmoth sucks the nectar from flowers while still in flight.

Brimstone: A small, pale yellow butterfly common to Europe. It is not unusual to see a great number of them drinking together from a puddle.

Burnet Moths: Any of several European species of the family Zygaenidae, some of which are active by day (diurnal), and others of which are active by night (nocturnal). The diurnal species have stocky bodies, gray back wings with red patches, and red front wings with a black border.

Burying Beetle: This beetle is so named because it buries the small, dead animals on which its larvae feeds.

Butterflies: see Lepidopterans.

Chrysalis: The stage of an insect's life in which the larva encloses itself in some form of protective covering while its transformation into its adult form takes place. The chrysalis is also called the pupa, cocoon, or nymph.

Chrysopide: The name of this green insect means "golden eye," and it has four large transparent wings. It is a useful insect because its larvae eat aphids.

344

As they search for nectar, butterflies help pollinate flowers as they take the pollen that sticks to their bodies from one flower to another.

Cicada: On hot summer days one can hear the buzzing whine of the male cicada's mating call. This sound is produced when it rubs together two membranes called timbals. The sound is amplified in the abdomen in two hollow cavities, like the soundbox of a guitar or violin.

Classification: The method used by scientists to group different animals having similarities. The animal

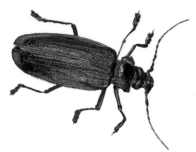

The titan beetle is one of the largest of all insects, but it is harmless.

kingdom is divided into phyla, the phyla into classes, and the classes into orders. The orders are divided into families, which in turn are subdivided into genera. Finally, genera are subdivided into the different individual animal or plant species.

Cockchafer: A member of the scarab beetle family, this common insect is very harmful. Adult cockchafers eat the leaves of trees while the larvae, which live in the ground, eat the roots.

The syrphid fly looks like a bee or a wasp, but has no stinger.

Cockroach: This very common insect has a flat body, which allows it to hide in narrow cracks. Cockroaches are found all over the world, especially in large cities, where they will often infest houses and apartments.

This leaf roller has golden flecks. Other species have different colors.

Coleopterans: Insects of the order Coleoptera, which includes most beetles. The majority live on land, but some live in the water. The front pair of wings of the coleopterans form a tough shell that covers the pair of wings used for flight.

Comma: A common butterfly found throughout Europe, the comma gets its unusual name from the white C-shape on the underside of the back wings.

Cricket: A smaller, darker colored relative of the grasshopper, crickets live on plants that are in bloom. On summer

Some species of bees build wax nests in the ground that house both their larvae and their food.

nights in the countryside, it is not uncommon to hear male crickets serenading females.

Dalla Caius: This rare butterfly's front wings are brown with yellow spots. Its back wings are yellow and black.

Dipterans: The order of insects that includes flies and mosquitoes. The dipteran has a single pair of wings, and it uses its mouth parts for sucking through a needle-like tube. Some of these insects transmit serious diseases such as yellow fever, malaria, or sleeping sickness.

Dragonfly: This insect has a very long, slender body, and one or two pairs of large wings. These wings enable it to fly very quickly and to hover in midair. It lives near ponds and streams, and its larva is aquatic.

Dung Beetle: Growing to not more than 1.5 in (3 cm) in length, the dung beetle gathers dung into a ball and rolls it backwards with its hind legs.

Earthworm: This annelid worm has a long body formed by many rings called

Fishermen consider the earthworm among the best bait.

metameres. If cut in half, this worm can regrow its tail end. Earthworms are extremely useful in the soil for aeration, and for helping to break down plant matter.

Earwig: When earwig larvae are born, the mother is careful that they do not wander too far, just like a human mother and her children. These insects, with their dangerous-looking pincers at the posterior end, are very common garden pests.

Elytron: Modified front wings that are not used for flying and that are found on many insects and beetles. Elytra are usually tough and leathery, occasionally having prickly horns, and function to protect the wings that are used for flying.

The brimstone gets its name from the bright yellow mineral of the same name, also known as sulfur.

The kallima inachus, or Indian leaf butterfly, has splendid colors on the upper part of its wings.

Emperor Moth: A nocturnal moth found in northern Africa, Asia Minor, and Europe. It has a wingspan of 5 to 6 in (14 to 16 cm).

Firefly: The male firefly has wings and it flies at night. The female does not have wings and lives on the ground. Both sexes give off a greenish light caused by a chemical reaction of two substances, luciferin and the enzyme luciferase.

Flea: A very small parasitic insect having a flattened body and no wings. Its strong back legs enable it to leap great distances. Fleas feed on the blood of mammals and can carry infectious diseases.

The necrophore, or burying beetle, buries small dead animals for its larvae to feed on.

Fritillary: This pretty butterfly has brown wings with white and orange markings. Its coloring varies greatly, however, according to the species.

Fruit Fly: Usually only a tenth of an inch (2 to 3 mm) long, the fruit fly is attracted to wine and fermented fruit. The fruit fly is often used in the study of genetics, which is the science of the transmission of hereditary features from parents to children. The fruit fly has a relatively simple genetic code.

Gastropods: Members of the mollusk group, which includes snails and slugs, and some other species that live in the water. Land gastropods can have either a shell (snails) or no shell (slugs). Both have no legs and they slither on their bellies.

Geometer Moth: A brownish or gray moth that comes out in the evening. Although the moth is not very energetic, the larva of the geometer, the inchworm, has an unusual way of moving. These caterpillars arch and extend their bodies, looking as though they are measuring out the distance they travel. The name geometer means "earth measurer."

In some countries, snails are considered a delicacy.

Golden Cetonian Beetle: A splendid green beetle with golden flecks. This beetle lives on sap from trees and on nectar from flower buds.

Grasshopper: These common jumping insects range in size from very small to nearly 6 in (15 cm) in length and come in many different colors. Certain species of grasshoppers form swarms of millions, devouring and destroying all crops and vegetation in their path.

The polyphilla fullo is an odd-looking beetle with tasselled antennae.

Special collars containing insecticides are used on pets to fight fleas.

Greenbottle Fly: The larva of this fly is parasitic; that is, it lives under the skin of larger, live host animals. However, because it feeds mostly on damaged tissues, the greenbottle fly promotes healing of the host.

Head Lice: These very small parasitic insects are considered a nuisance. Lice nest in the hair and scalp, feeding on the host's blood. An infestation of lice is called pediculosis. Lice can transmit diseases from one host to another.

Unlike butterflies, moths are nocturnal and are generally quite slow-moving and easy to catch.

Hercules Beetle: Named after the mythological hero of the twelve labors, this beetle can grow to a length of 6.5 in (17 cm). By day it hides in decaying wood and by night it crawls on the ground or flies with difficulty.

Hornet: A relative of the wasp and bee, the hornet also has a stinger and flies from flower to flower in search of nectar. It usually builds its nest underground.

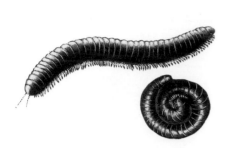

When resting, the millipede rolls itself into a coil.

Horsefly: This member of the order Diptera is related to the fly. Males feed on liquids and flower nectar, while the females take blood from mammals and humans.

House Fly: This dipteran is found worldwide except for polar regions. The larvae, called maggots, do not have feet or antennae. They move like worms, and live and feed on decaying matter. The adult feeds primarily on liquids. Humans and large animals alike wage a constant war to get rid of these pesky insects.

Hummingbird Hawkmoth: This butterfly has a stocky body, can fly at speeds in excess of 30 mph (50 km/h), and can hover in midair like a hummingbird. Its Latin name means "long tongue."

Hymenoptera: This order of insects typically has membranous wings and includes bees, wasps, and ants. These insects are useful to humans because they eat harmful pests, pollinate flowers, and provide us with honey.

Silverfish are a household pest that are sometimes found in old books.

Indian Leaf Butterfly: This butterfly of the Himalayas and central China gives a beautiful display of color when its wings are open. When it lands, the brownish color of its wings allow the Indian leaf butterfly to blend into its surroundings.

Insect: Small invertebrate animals in the class Insecta, an extremely diverse group that has over a million different species. An adult insect's body has three segments: head, thorax, and abdomen. It has a pair of antennae and six legs. Some insects do not have wings, others have one or more pairs. Insects emerge from eggs and, through a process of change called metamorphosis, are transformed into their adult form.

Ladybug: This very common, red spotted beetle is a very useful insect. The ladybug eats aphids, which destroy roses and many important crops. If you

Small apollo butterflies prefer the cool, mountain climate.

have a ladybug on your hand and point a finger upwards, the ladybug will go up to the tip. It will then open its wings and, after hesitating a moment, fly away.

Larva: The first stage of life of an insect after hatching from an egg. During this worm-like, wingless stage, the insect is already independent, and spends its time feeding itself and growing. They remain in this stage until the pupa or chrysalis stage. Various kinds of larvae are also known as caterpillars, grubs and maggots. The larva usually looks very different from the adult form.

Leaf Roller: This weevil is named for its habit of rolling tree leaves into a cigar shape. It uses these leaves as a home for its eggs and larvae. The leaf roller's long snout or proboscis, which is characteristic of weevils, gives it an unusual appearance.

Lepidopterans: The order of insects that includes moths and butterflies. Lepidopterans have wings covered by often very colorful, microscopic scales.

The greenbottle fly is named for its coloring.

Long-Horned Beetle: At nearly 2 in (5 cm) long, this insect's antennae are almost twice as long as its body. The female lays her eggs in cracks on living trees, and the larvae cause considerable damage.

Mayfly: This insect lives near fresh water in most parts of the world. The mayfly is recognized by its two pairs of large, transparent, delicately veined wings.

Metamorphosis: The complete change in structure that some animals, such as insects and amphibians, undergo in order to attain their adult form. With insects, it is the transformation from the larval stage into the dormant pupae or chrysalis stage, followed by the emergence of the winged adult.

The coffee bean borer is a serious pest on coffee bean plantations.

Millipede: This insect has only about 400 feet, not quite 1,000 as its name suggests. The millipede hides in dark, damp areas, and feeds on decaying plant matter.

Mimicry: Many animals assume forms and colors that blend in with their environment in order to hide from predators. Some harmless species mimic the coloring of a dangerous species. For example, we are wary of the harmless syrphid fly because it looks like a bee.

Mole Cricket: As its name suggests, the mole cricket lives underground. It digs long chambers with its strong forelegs. The larvae develop in the ground, eating roots and other plant matter.

Mosquito: Who is not familiar with this pest? Only the females suck the blood of humans and other animals. Components in the blood are required for the maturation of mosquito eggs. The larvae are small aquatic creatures that are shaped like a comma. They develop in stagnant water.

The '89' butterfly, or figure-of-eight, is named for the pattern on its wings. It is a member of the Nymphalidae family.

Moth: The clothes moth feeds on woolen and fur garments. The mill moth prefers grains, flour, and pasta.

Notodontids: A large family of small- to medium-sized moths found world-wide. Many species have a tuft of scales on the edge of their wings. When the wings are folded, the tufts stand out, hence the name of several species called 'prominents.' The larval caterpillars are quite hairless, and often have grotesque humps and spines.

Nymph: Another name for a pupa or chrysalid.

Nymphalids: A family of very beautiful and colorful butterflies that includes the peacock butterfly, which has two large eyespots on its wings.

Peacock Butterfly: The black, hairy, and not very attractive pupa transforms into one of the most beautiful European butterflies. The upper side of the wing is very brightly colored with patches of intense color that resemble eyes.

In the summer, goldsmith beetles are often seen on roses.

Pill-Millipede, or Sow Bug: This small insect is related to the millipede and is often found in damp places and under rocks. If disturbed, it rolls itself into a ball so that its attacker cannot get hold of it.

Potato Beetle: This is one of the most harmful insects to farmers because it eats the leaves of the potato plant. The potato beetle looks like a large yellowish ladybug with black stripes. This insect is a native of North America, but arrived in Europe during the 19th century.

Praying Mantis: This predator insect is named for the praying position in which it holds its front legs. The praying mantis grasps its prey with its long prickly legs and devours it. This is often the fate of the male after it has mated with the female.

The swallowtail butterfly has tail-like extensions on its back wings

Proboscis: The long tubelike mouthparts of certain insects. The proboscis of a butterfly is a long tube that is uncurled to suck nectar from the corolla of a flower.

Red Admiral Butterfly: This butterfly has black wings with brick-red and white patches. Its larva is grayish-black and it lives on nettles.

Scarab Beetle: The name of several diverse types of coleoptera. Scarabs often have very specific forms and males generally have metallic coloration.

Scorpion: This relative of the spider is an arachnid, not an insect. The young develop inside the mother and are born live. They stay with their mother, perched on her back, until their first molt (shedding of skin). Most scorpions are poisonous and their sting is very painful.

Black cockroaches often nest in old houses.

Silkworm: Along with the bee, this is the insect most frequently raised by humans. It produces the silk threads used to make silk fabric. The larvae are raised in mulberry bushes, which is their favorite food. The larvae then wrap themselves in a cocoon made out of very fine silk threads. The cocoons are harvested, and then the silky fibers are separated and spun into threads.

Silverfish: These small, harmless insects have no wings and are silver in color. They live under the bark of trees, under rocks in the woods, and also in houses.

Beware of wasps! Their sting is very painful.

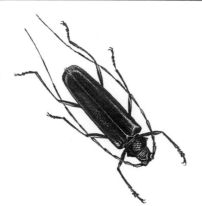

The long-horned beetle has antennae up to 4 in (10 cm) in length.

Small Apollo: This butterfly has white wings with small black markings. The lower, or posterior, wings also have red marks edged in black with a white spot in the middle.

Snail: This animal is a mollusk of the class of gastropods, which are invertebrate animals that slither on a muscular organ called a foot and that give off a slimy substance. When it is disturbed, the snail pulls back into its shell. There are retractable antennae on the front of its head, and its eyes are located on one pair of these antennae.

Spider: Although often called an insect, the spider is actually an arachnid, a class that also includes scorpions, ticks, and mites. Although most spiders pose little or no danger to humans, these eight-legged creatures

The markings on the wings of the emperor moth resemble eyes.

arouse great fear, which is usually unjustified. In fact, spiders perform a very useful service by capturing large numbers of harmful and even dangerous insects. Spiders spin webs made of very fine but strong silk, which they use to trap their prey.

Stick Insect: This well-camouflaged insect hides in the branches of bushes. In fact, it looks so much like a dry twig that it can be detected only when it moves.

Swallowtail Butterfly: This common butterfly has yellow wings that have black markings and a black-bordered, blue stripe along the edges. The back wings have tail-like extensions with red patches.

Syrphid Fly: A family of delicate flies resembling bees or wasps, but lacking a stinger. They are not harmful to humans and are useful because they feed on aphids.

Tachnid Fly: This strange-looking fly has a short, hairy body. While harmless to humans, this fly's larvae penetrate the nests of other insects, such as the wasp, and eat the food that is intended for the host larvae. When that food is finished, this insect then eats the host larvae.

Termite: These insects belong to the order Isoptera, and, like ants, they live in very large colonies with each member having a specific task. The queen is the

In the summer, female horseflies feed on the blood of humans and animals.

only fertile female and becomes so large that she cannot move. Termites eat and burrow in wood, and can cause considerable damage to buildings.

Titan Beetle: Named after the titans, the giants of Greek mythology, this beetle is the giant of all insects. It grows up to 6 in (15 cm) in length. It lives in the forests of Brazil and Guyana, and feeds on vegetation.

Tsetse Fly: This African fly carries and transmits a deadly disease called sleeping sickness. For this reason, the tsetse fly is studied closely by scientists.

Underwing Moth: This large nocturnal moth grows to 3 in (7 cm) long. During the day, the grayish color of its front wings helps it to hide on tree trunks where it rests. If disturbed, it will fly away quickly, exposing the bright red of its posterior wings.

The larva of a Notodontid moth. Its name means "tooth on the back."

Wasp: These hymenopterans have a stinger that injects a very painful venom. Wasps live in nests made of paper, which they produce themselves. They feed on sweet liquids such as flower nectar and fruit juices.

Water Beetle: This aquatic coleopteran is a voracious predator of other insects, their larvae, and even small fish and tadpoles. Its two back legs are used as oars to swim about underwater. Water beetles must come to the surface to breathe, and they carry a bubble of air with them as they swim.

Weevil: One of the most common coleopteran beetles, thousands of different types of weevils are found the world over in many different sizes. They have a very long head that tapers into a long nose, called a proboscis. They are considered very destructive because they eat leaves and bore into grains, nuts, and flowers.

Woodworm: A small, cylindrical coleopteran, the woodworm feeds on different types of vegetation, but prefers dry, dead wood.

Drawn by the light, the underwing moth is often found in homes.

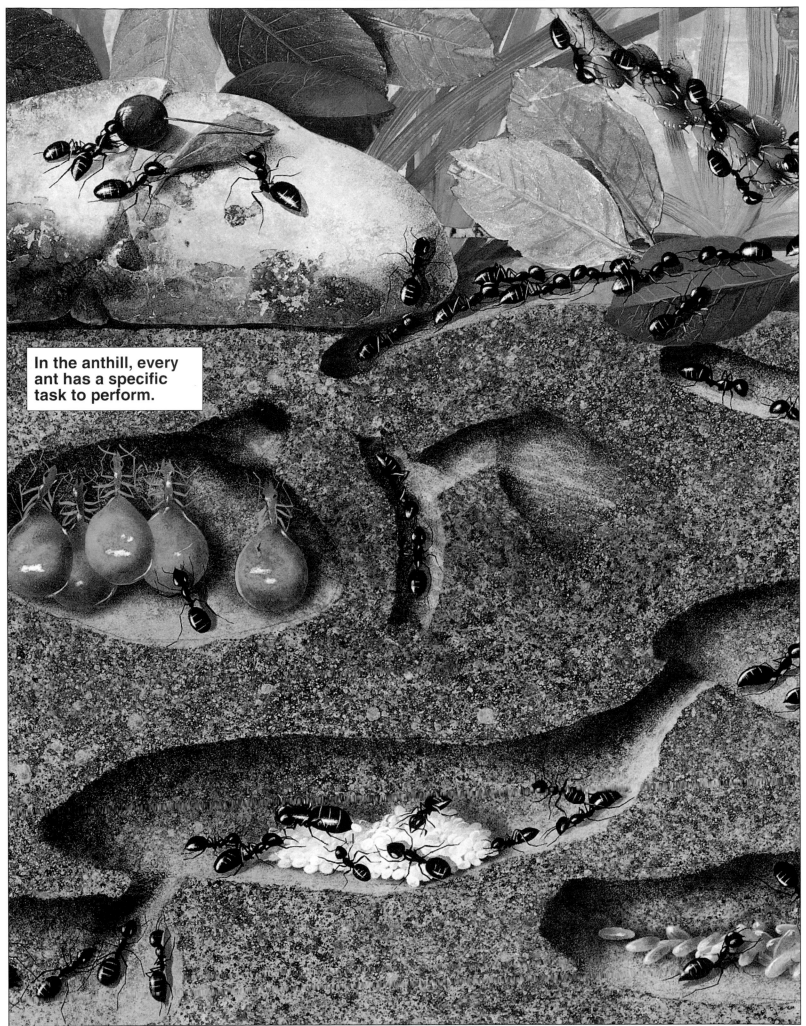

In the anthill, every ant has a specific task to perform.

Biological Control: A process used in agriculture as an alternative to pesticides. Insects that carry disease or destroy crops can be controlled by introducing into their environment other organisms that are their natural enemies. For example, in tree plantations, foresters set up nesting boxes to attract certain birds that eat insects that feed on wood.

Many marine species have become extinct because of water pollution.

Biosphere: The relatively small part of the earth's crust and atmosphere in which life can be sustained.

CFC: The abbreviation for chlorofluoro-carbons, which are artificial substances used in various manufacturing methods and consumer products. CFCs are one of the main causes of the destruction of the ozone layer, which is a layer of atmospheric gas that surrounds the earth, protecting it from harmful ultraviolet rays.

Chemistry: The science that studies the properties and structures of all natural and artificial substances. In ecologists' language, the word "chemical" is negative, and refers to substances that are artificial and therefore not in harmony with natural laws.

Recycling paper helps cut down the demand for pulpwood and thus saves trees.

Chernobyl: A city in the Ukraine and the site of a nuclear reactor plant that was devastated by an enormous nuclear accident in 1986. Even today, the environment and people that were involved either directly or indirectly in this ecological disaster continue to suffer terrible consequences.

China Syndrome: The fear of nuclear disaster. The term was coined in a 1979 American movie that depicted a nuclear disaster in the United States and its repercussions in China.

Civilization: The sum of every aspect of human culture. Thus, we can speak of Egyptian civilization, Roman civilization, industrial civilization, as well as the Plains Indians' civilization, Inuit civilization, and Australian aboriginal civilization.

Climate: The specific metereologic conditions (winds, rain, snow, hours of sunlight, temperatures, etc.) of a given region of the Earth.

The bicycle is an environmentally-friendly means of transportation because it does not pollute.

Compost: A mixture of decomposed vegetable matter and organic waste used as fertilizer.

Composting: The process of "recycling" or decomposing fruit and vegetable scraps, hay, leaves, and other organic wastes into soil fertilizer.

Conservation: The protection, preservation, and careful management of natural resources, plants, animals, the environment, and natural habitats.

Consumerism: The philosophy that human activity should strive towards economic wealth through the buying and selling of more and more goods. Advertising promotes the desire to buy and to have bigger, better, and more attractive goods, many of which are quite useless and unnecessary.

DDT: A highly effective, but toxic insecticide. DDT was used for many years to kill the mosquitos that carry malaria. The harmful effects on human health as well as on the environment were unknown at the time it was used. It was finally banned in North America and Europe at the end of the 1960s. It is still used in many developing countries.

Developing Country: A country that has not attained a standard of living comparable to that found in Europe and North America. Generally, the inhabitants of developing countries are involved in farming to feed themselves.

This satellite is powered by solar energy.

These people are often poor and can die of hunger in difficult times if no governmental support is offered. The level of education in these countries is often low and the population high.

Development Model: An alternative plan developed and to be followed, consciously or subconsciously, by every human society for the betterment of all life on Earth. It concerns all fields of human study and endeavor from technology to ethics. The model works only when all forms of life are respected.

Ecological: Referring to something that does no harm to the environment, or that promotes a respect for nature and for ecology.

Ecologist: A scientist who studies ecology.

Ecology: The science that studies the relationship between organisms and their environments.

Ecosystem: The sum of the living organisms and of non-living or inorganic elements (solar energy, soil and minerals, air, water) of an environment. For example, a pond with its specific plants, animals, water, bottom soil, sunlight, and air mixture is considered an ecosystem.

Environment: All that surrounds us—air, water, plants, animals, earth, minerals—in which life finds physical and biological support.

Thanks to green chlorophyll, plants change sunlight into energy.

Environmental Degradation or Breakdown: The result of the damage caused by humans to the environment and to life, in their various forms. Environmental degradation is usually caused by the combined effect of small amounts of damage done by individuals. For example, the engine of one car causes an imperceptible increase in air pollution levels, but, when multiplied by tens of thousands of cars, the air becomes dangerously polluted.

Environmental Impact: The effects of human activity on the environment. Experts are often able to project and predict these effects before the activity has begun by using a process known as environmental impact assessment.

Environmentalism: The philosophy that encourages people to protect nature and to safeguard endangered species and environments at risk.

Eolian Energy: The energy obtained from the wind. Eolian energy is generally electric power that comes from rotating turbines inside large windmills. The adjective eolian comes from Eolo, who was the Greek god of the winds.

Eutrophication: The natural process that provides the nutrients required to maintain the vital functions of organisms that live in an aquatic environment. Pollution affects this process by causing some nutrients to flourish and others to greatly diminish, a process that can determine the survival of certain species over others.

Extinction: A relatively common process in the natural world and the result of the failure of a life-form to adapt to changing environmental conditions. It is not in itself a negative thing. Extinction is considered negative if its causes are not related to long-term natural phenomena, but instead are caused by the irresponsible acts of humans. Examples are pollution, over-hunting, or the destruction of an

Eolian energy is produced by windmills that turn turbines.

animal's natural habitat, such as the logging of the rain forests.

Food Chain: The arrangement of organisms according to the order in which one species preys on another. Plants are the first link in the chain (primary producers), then the herbivores (primary consumers or secondary producers), and finally the carnivores (secondary consumers).

Food Web: The complex interrelationship between the producers and the consumers in all the food chains within an ecosystem.

Forest: A dense growth of trees that consists of a whole community of plants having close ecological ties with one another, and with the soil in which they grow, the animals living there, and the climate. Forests grow over a vast area, and forest plants grow to various heights. Most mosses

Plastic, glass, and aluminum can be recycled. Trash to be recycled should be sorted according to what it is made of.

and lichens grow at the soil level, herbaceous plants and shrubs grow somewhat taller. The leaves of small trees often form a canopy that is almost impenetrable by sunlight. Mature trees extend above the canopy.

Fossil Energy: The energy obtained by burning fossil fuels: oil, coal, and natural gas. Unlike eolian, geothermal, solar, and water energy, fossil fuels are a nonrenewable energy source because, at the present rate of consumption, they will eventually be used up.

Fossil Fuels: Substances that originate from subterranean deposits of fossilized organic material, which, when burned, release energy. Oil, coal, and natural gas are examples. These fuels are said to be non-renewable, since no more can be easily created once the underground reserves are emptied.

Gaia: In ancient Greek, Gaia means Mother Earth. According to the Gaia hypothesis, an alternative philosophy, the Earth is a single, large, living organism capable of intelligent response to feedback from everything that lives on it.

Geothermal Energy: The energy that is obtained from tapping the heat contained in the magma beneath the Earth's crust. Geothermal energy is easily obtained only in volcanic regions of the world.

Global: That which concerns the entire globe, or all of the Earth.

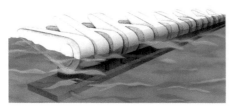

This equipment uses the movement of waves to produce energy.

Green: A term used to describe something that is natural or environmentally-friendly. It is also used to describe the political movement that promotes the ideal of sustainable development.

Greenhouse Effect: The theory that the temperature of the Earth's atmosphere and surface is increasing due to human activity. Industry, cars, and the intensive raising of livestock causes the production of gases such as carbon dioxide, methane, nitrogen oxide, and ozone. These gases accumulate in the atmosphere and trap the heat from the sun's rays in the same manner that a greenhouse's glass covering keeps heat inside. On a global scale, the greenhouse effect is said to be responsible for sudden changes in the climate.

This model power station uses the temperature difference between water on the sea floor and water at the surface to produce energy.

Greenpeace: An organization dedicated to the protection of the environment. Established in the 1970s, Greenpeace is well known for its often spectacular protests, such as the occupation of areas in which nuclear bomb testing is planned. Its more active members are called "rainbow warriors."

Health: The absence of illness or pain. According to one development model (see entry), health results when one lives in an unpolluted environment.

Hydroelectric Energy: The energy obtained from the force of water. Due to its abundance and its "clean," or low pollution value, hydroelectric energy is called "white coal." Even so, to obtain this energy often has a serious negative impact on the environment.

Plants can also grow in nutrient solutions (hydroponics).

The construction of large dams creates artificial lakes that devastate vast portions of the countryside. Scientists and engineers are attempting to develop other less harmful ways of generating hydroelectric energy, such as by using the tidal forces of the oceans.

Imbalance: The result of an unusual increase of one or more organisms in an environment through the introduction of factors of disturbance. These factors can be pollutants, species from other continents, or artificial changes.

Litter: The layer of dead leaves covering the forest floor. Litter contains bacteria, fungi, and small invertebrates, which help to decompose organic matter. Litter constitutes a miniature, complex food chain. In the human world, litter is solid waste garbage that has been left on the ground and not recycled or disposed of properly.

Mother Earth: A term used to emphasize the special relationship—similar to that between a mother and her child—between every living being, including humans, and the planet. See also "Gaia."

Nature: All things and beings of the universe. More specifically, all that occurs naturally on Earth.

In autumn, the production of green chlorophyll in leaves stops, and the plants lose their leaves.

Nuclear or Atomic Energy: The energy derived from the decomposition of radioactive materials. Nuclear energy is generally obtained from uranium, a radioactive element that "breaks down" into other elements. This process produces radioactive particles, heat, and neutrons. These in turn strike other uranium atoms, which split, triggering an extremely violent chain reaction. Nuclear energy is considered a clean form of energy since it produces steam only as an immediate by-product of generating electricity. In reality, however, nuclear waste,

The Siberian tiger is an endangered species.

which is the fuel that is no longer sufficiently productive, remains highly radioactive for thousands of years, and it is difficult to dispose of it. This waste may create terrible hazards for future generations. Furthermore, nuclear power plants are extremely costly to build and to run due to the sophistication of the equipment that is required in the creation of a controlled nuclear reaction. An accident at a nuclear plant (see "Chernobyl") can have a disastrous effect on people, plants, and animals in a huge area surrounding the plant.

Hot and cold environments are host to different animals. In order to survive, these animals have adapted to the environmental conditions of their habitats.

Organic Energy: The energy released by the burning of renewable materials such as wood or peat. This very basic form of energy production is still used today in many parts of the world. The use of large amounts of wood is the cause of the deforestation of vast regions of Asia and Africa.

Organic: An adjective having many meanings that, in one way or another, relate to life and to living organisms. In everyday language, this word is used to indicate products derived from the natural processes involving living organisms. It also means foods that are grown and harvested without the use of artificial fertilizers and pesticides. In chemistry, it indicates any compound containing carbon. In biology, it refers to the organs of the body.

Ozone: A gas, very similar to oxygen, that forms a layer in the stratosphere. The ozone layer serves to shield Earth from the harmful ultraviolet rays of the sun. Atmospheric pollution and the use of products such as chlorofluorocarbons (see "CFC") have created a hole in the ozone layer over Antarctica.

Pesticides: Chemical products used in agriculture in the battle against pests. Among the most common are herbicides, which are used against plants that infest crops; fungicides, which are used against fungi that cause diseases; and insecticides, which are used against harmful insects. The massive use of pesticides causes pollution of the soil and water, and the disappearance of some species of animals and plants.

Pollution: The release of waste products into the environment.

Recycling: The process by which waste materials can be transformed into something useful. Recycling requires the collection of garbage that has been sorted according to different types of material, such as paper, aluminum, or plastic. These materials must be placed into separate containers.

Renewable Resource: Anything that can be naturally replenished. Trees,

Hiking is a recreational activity that brings people in touch with nature.

for example, can be encouraged to grow where other trees have been cut down for use as wood.

Resource: A naturally occurring material or source of energy.

Solar Energy: The most important source of energy for the Earth. Every day, thanks to the sun, plants are able to produce sugars, which are a form of stored chemical energy, from carbon dioxide and water. The rest of the food chain is dependent on this chemical energy. Solar energy is also captured by humans using special materials and carefully constructed solar collectors to produce electricity.

To plant a tree is to start a new life.

Sustainable Development: Any type of development by a society that does not have an irreversible impact on the natural resources or the health of the environment. Sustainable development keeps the equilibrium found in nature intact.

Symbiosis: The ecological relationship between two species in which both species benefit. For example, the stinging tentacles of the sea anemone protect the hermit crab, which in turn carries the sea anemone about helping it to find its food.

Technology: The application of knowledge for a practical purpose. This is an ability of the human species in particular. Technology applies the ideas and theories put forward by science.

Christmas trees are also sold as live plants in soil so that they can be transplanted later.

Trojan Horse: After ten years of seige and war, the ancient Greeks, as Homer tells us, had not yet managed to conquer the city of Troy. So Ulysses had a large wooden horse built in which many soldiers hid. The Greeks then pretended to leave, giving up the attack. The Trojans, believing that the

In one of La Fontaine's fables, a chicken lays golden eggs for his greedy master.

horse was a farewell gift, brought it into their city. That night, the Greeks came out of the wooden horse and conquered Troy.

Tweety: The famous yellow canary in the Warner Brothers cartoons and comic strips. Tweety Bird's cage is always open, and Sylvester the cat is forever trying to catch him, but he never succeeds.

The Ugly Duckling: The fairy tale by Hans Christian Andersen in which a

In this fable, the stork gets even with the fox for playing a trick on it.

swan's egg is accidentally hatched by a duck. Being uglier and more awkward than the other ducklings from birth, it is treated with suspicion by its brothers and all the other animals on the farm. The poor little "duckling" feels different and, because the others are teasing him, he runs away. After many adventures, he comes upon a pond inhabited by beautiful swans. Seeing his reflection in the water, he discovers that he is one of them.

Unicorn: This mythical animal looks like a horse with a single long horn on its forehead. It also has the hind legs of a stag, a goat's beard, and a lion's tail. The unicorn is a symbol of chastity.

Werewolf: A frightening character of literature and horror films. A werewolf is a person who turns into a wolf on nights when the moon is full. The legend of the werewolf may have some scientific basis, since the phases of the moon seem to affect the moods and behavior of humans and animals, as well as the growth of crops and the movement of the tides.

White Fang: The wolf that is the main character in Jack London's 1906 novel of the same name. The story takes place in Alaska during the gold rush and tells of the friendship between a wolf and a gold prospector.

Dragons are mythical animals found in fables and legends in both Europe and the Far East.

White Rabbit: In Lewis Carroll's novel *Alice's Adventures in Wonderland* (1865), Alice follows a white rabbit down a hole and meets some unusual talking animals: an indignant mouse; a dodo bird; a lorikeet; Bill the lizard; a newborn baby who turns into a pig; the Cheshire Cat who fades in and out; the March Hare; flamingos that serve as croquet mallets and hedgehogs that are used as croquet balls; and the gryphon with the head and wings of an eagle and the body of a lion. At the end of the book, Alice wakes up, suggesting that the story was all a dream.

Wile E. Coyote: The coyote of the Warner Brothers television cartoons who is always trying to catch the Road Runner. Naturally, he never succeeds.

The Fox and the Crow is one of La Fontaine's best-loved fables.

Willy: A killer whale in the feature-length movie *Free Willy*. Willy lives in an aquarium and at the end of the movie is freed into the ocean. The trained killer whale used in the film is named Keiko. Keiko was captured at the age of two off the coast of Iceland.

Winnie the Pooh: The honey-loving toy bear who is the main character in storybooks by English writer A. A. Milne, illustrated by E. H. Shepard. Pooh has many stuffed toy friends—Rabbit, Piglet, Owl, Tigger, Roo and his mother Kanga, the donkey Eeyore, and a boy named Christopher Robin. Walt Disney later produced an animated movie version of the famous Pooh stories.

Wolf: Wolves are common characters in fairy tales. Perhaps the most well known is the wolf who eats the grandmother in Perrault's *Little Red Riding Hood*. The Brothers Grimm created the wolf that chases the three little pigs, but who is finally outsmarted by them.

"Let me cross!" "No, I'm crossing." Soon the two stubborn goats fall off the bridge in this classic fable.

Index

INDEX

This index is arranged in alphabetical order.
The words in **boldface type** show you the title
of a page in which a subject is treated in depth.

A

abalone 253
aboriginal population 352
acid rain 352
Aconcagua, Mount 49
acorn 72, 95
Adams, Richard 360
adaptation 352
addax 171
adder 340
adipose fin 312
Adventures of Pinocchio 364
Aesculapian snake 338
Aesop 360, 362, 367
African Animals, Classifications 300-303
African Forests 196-201
African Rocky Deserts 174-177
African Sandy Deserts 172-173
agouara 121
agouti, golden 121
Akela 360
albatross 20, 27, 307, 326
Alice's Adventures in Wonderland 367, 368
Alice shad 325
alligator, American 184, 187, 338
alpaca 49, 51
Alps 60-63
amanita 93
Amazon Forest 190-194
Amazon River 108, 191
amberjack 250
Amphibians 342, 338-343
amphipod, eyeless 99
amphiuma, two-toed 343
anaconda 191, 194, 338, 342
anadromous 312

anchovy 232
Andersen, Hans Christian 360, 362, 363
Andes 48-49
angelfish 228, 245, 256
    imperial 256
    ringed 245
anglerfish 241, 243
anhinga 187
annelids 344
ant 344, 351
    leaf-cutting 191, 193
Antarctica 26-27, 14, 15, 29
Antarctica, Animal Classifications 304-307
anteater
    giant 121, 123, 289
    spiny 147, 149, 304
Antelope 134-135
    four-horned 53, 55, 297
    Indian 297
    royal 135
    Tibetan 57
antennae 344
anthropocentric 352
anthropomorphism 352
antlers 37, 88-89
ant lion 344
anubis 360
anura 342
apatura iris 344
ape, Barbary 294
aphids 344
apis 360
Aquarium 256, 312
aquarium keeping 312
arachnids 344
araponga 326, 328
archaeopteryx 326
archerfish 213, 312

Arctic Circle 18
Arctic Regions 14-17
Argali 53, **59,** 295
Argentina 121
Argo 360
Aristocats 360
armadillo 121
    giant 121, 288
    nine-banded 193
artificial 352
Asian Animals, Classifications 295-299
Asian Big Cats 219
Asian Jungle 212-216
asp 292
    horned 340
atoll 246
atomic energy 356
Australia, Animals of, 148-149, 167
Australian Steppes 168-169
avocet 326
aye-aye 211

B

Babar 360
Babe 362
badger 73
    American 179
    European 91, 292
Bagheera 362
bald eagle 285, 326
baleen 235
Baloo 362
Baltimore oriole 326, 337
Bambi 362
banyan (tree) 214
baobab (tree) 127
barbel 108, 312, 319

Mediterranean 319
barnacles 251
barreleye, deep-sea 241, 243
basilisk 338, 342
bass 250
  largemouth 323
  sea 312, 316, 325
Bast 280, 362
bat 99
  long-eared 99
  vampire 49
batfish 245, 312, 317
bat star 250
Bayard 362
beagle 278
bear
  Asiatic black 53, 54
  black 75
  Brown 70, 91, 94, **102-103,**
    292
  grizzly 45, 46, 73, 75, 285
  Malay 298
  Polar 17, **18-19,** 284
  spectacled 50, 288
  sun 298
Beauty and the Beast 362
Beaver 71, 75, **78-79,** 287
bee 107, 344, 346
beetle
  bathysciola 99
  blind 99
  blind rhadinid 99
  burying 344, 347
  carabus 106
  carabus auronitens 106
  dung 346
  golden 344
  golden cetonian 347
  goldsmith 106, 107, 349
  Hercules 347
  long-horned 348, 350
  potato 349
  scarab 349, 366
  titan 346, 350
  water 321, 350
beluga 235
benthos 242
bicycle 352
bighorn 46, 47, 285
bilby 169, 305
biocentric 352
biodegradable 352
biodynamics 352

biological control 354
biosphere 354
bird feeder 104
bird of paradise 157, 304, 327
bird watching 104
Birds 326-337
  Amazon 195
  Arctic 24-25
  Asian Jungle 224
  European 104-105
  Farmyard 275
  Oceanian 156-157
  Tundra 36
Bison
  American 115, 116, **118-119,**
    287
  European 119
blackbird 275, 328, 335
blackbuck 165, 216, 297
bleak 321
blenny, freshwater 312, 321
blind-worm 106, 338
blueberries 103
boa constrictor 338
boa, rainbow 191, 193
boar
  crested wild 299
  European 91, 126
bobac 163
bobcat 83, 116, 179, 180, 287
bobtail 277
bongo 198
booby 328
bream 250
  gilthead sea 313, 317
  sea 316
brimstone (butterfly) 344, 346
bristlemouth
  cyclothone 241
  deep-sea 243
  vinciguerra 243
Bucephalus 362, 366
Buck 362, 366
Buffalo 115
  African 127, **129,** 303
Buffalo Bill 116
Bugs Bunny 362
bullfrog 343
bumblebee 107
bunting 328
  snow 31, 336
burbot 323
bustard

great 163, 165, 341
little 163
butterfly 344, 345, 348
  blue 107
  blue morpho 193
  brimstone 344, 346
  cabbage 107
  comma 344, 346
  fritillary 347
  Indian leaf 347, 348
  mocker swallowtail 211
  peacock 349
  polygonia 344
  red admiral 107, 349
  small apollo 61, 348, 350
  swallowtail 107, 349, 350
  tortoise shell 107
butterflyfish 245, 312, 315
  forceps 247
buzzard 91, 328

C

cabbageworm 107
cactus 180, 181
Cactus Country 180-181
caddis fly worm 319
caecilian 341
caiman, black 338
calf 259, 264
Caligula's horse 362
Call of the Wild 362, 365, 366
calling hare 45, 75
camel 164
  Bactrian 163, 164, 297
  dromedary 171, 172, 300
camouflage 36, 85, 128, 197, 209
Canada 75, 76
Canadian Forests 74-77
canary 282, 310, 328, 335, 336
capercaillie, European 43, 61,
    291
capuchin
  black-capped 191
  white-faced 191
capybara 121, 192
caracara 331
cardinal 85, 328
cariama, crested 195
caribou 31, 37, 284
carp 108, 323
  crucian 323
  grass 325

Lake Garda 323
    mirror 323
cassowary 157, 306, 328
Cat and the Fox 362
Cat 259, 261, **280-281,** 310
    African tiger 197
    bicolor Persian 281
    British shorthair tabby, 281
    Cornish rex 281
    Egyptian tabby 280
    fishing 219, 299
    Manx 281
    native 305
    Pallas's 163
    red Persian 281
    Siamese 280
    Sphinx 281
    tabby 281
    viverrine 299
catadromous 312
caterpillar, swallowtail 107
catfish 175, 213, 323
Caves 99
Centaurs 362
centipede, brown 99
Cerberus 363
cercopithecus 197, 199, 200
Cetaceans 231, **234-237**
CFC 354
chaffinch 328, 329
    mountain 61
chaja 121
Challenger Deep 232
chameleon 175, 176, 338
    Jackson's 341
chamois 42, 61, 62, 64, 291
char 319
Cheetah 112, 113, 128, **138-139,**
        300, 363
    royal 139
chemistry 354
Chernobyl 354
chick 259, 260, 262, 328
chicken 262, 308
Chicken Coop 260, **262-263,**
chihuahua 276
Chimera 363, 366
Chimpanzee 185, **206-207,** 301
China Syndrome 354
chinchilla 49, 285
Chip and Dale 363
chiru 57
chrysalis 344

chrysopide 344
chub 321
cicada 346
cichlids 312
City Mouse and Country
        Mouse 362
civet
    Indian 215, 299
    palm 214, 215, 298
civilization 354
clam 253, 325
    giant 245
Classifications 283-310, 346
climate 354
clownfish 313
coati, brown-nosed 49
cobra 338
    hooded 340
    Indian 214
    king 213
Cockatoo 148, **158-159**
    black 159
    sulphur-crested 158, 159, 307
cockchafer 346
cocker 276
cockle 253
cockroach 346, 349
coelacanth 243
coffee bean borer 348
Cold Climates 14-15
coleopterans 346
collie 277
columbine 42
comet, red-tailed 49
compost, composting 354
condor 49, 50
    Andean 50, 288, 326
conservation 354
consumerism 354
coot 329
coral 245, 251
Coral Reefs 244-245, 246-247
cordon bleu 329, 337
corella, little 167
cormorant 229
    great 331
cottonmouth 187
cottontail 85, 86
cougar 75, 182
Cow 259, 260, **264-265,** 308
    Frisian 265
cowrie 249
Coyote 113, 115, **117,** 287

crab 254, 255
    fiddler 255
    hermit 249, 255
    spiny spider 255
crane 329, 367
    crowned 126, 300
    gray 335
crayfish 108, 319
cricket 106, 346, 362, 363
    mole 106, 349
Crocodile 204-205, 213, 338, 339
    dwarf 338
    Nile 200, 300, 341
    Osborn's dwarf 205
    saltwater 340
crossbill 329
crow 75, 275, 329
    carrion 91
Crustaceans 254-255
cuckoo 329
curlew 329
cuscus 147
    spotted 151, 304
cuttlefish 249, 252, 313, 315
cyclothone 243

D

dace 108, 321, 323
dachshund 276
    wire-haired 279
Daffy Duck 363
Dalla Caius 346
dandelion 106
Dane
    Great 276, 279
    Harlequin 279
Darma 363
DDT 354
Death Valley 180
Deep Sea 241-243
Deer 86, **88-89**
    European 61, 71
    fallow 91
    musk 55, 296
    pampas 121, 123
    red 91, 293
    roe 91, 92, 292
    white-tailed 85, 187
dentex 250
Deserts, Rocky 176-177
Deserts, Sandy 172-173
developing country 354

development model 354
dingo 167, 168, 304
dipterans 346
diver 243
diving-suit 243
doberman pinscher 279
dodo 329, 334
Dogmatix 363
Dogs 259, 261, **276-279,** 310
   Cape hunting 113
   hunting 278
   Sled Dogs 35
dolphin 231, 234, 237, 294
Domestic Animals,
     Classifications 308-310
Donald Duck 363
Donkeys 268, 308
dormouse 73, 93, 293
dory 108, 313, 315
dove 275
   bleeding-heart 328, 329
   collared 334
down 329
dragon 363, 368
   flying 340
   Komodo 341
dragonfish, boa 241, 243
dragonfly 109, 346
dromedary 171, 172, 300
Duck 105, **274,** 309, 329
   eider 331
   mallard 105, 110, 213, 274,
     292, 325, 333
   mandarin 213
Duck-Billed Platypus 154, 147,
   306
duckling, 259
duiker
   banded, 197
   blue 125
Durrell, Gerald 363

E

eagle 64, 67
   bald 76, 187
   bateleur 326, 334
   golden 45, 61, 63, 75, 291, 330
   sea 335
   steppes 163, 164, 336
   wedge-tailed 305
earthworm 106, 346
earwig 344, 346

ecological 354
ecologist 355
Ecology 42, 355, **352-359**
ecosystem 355
edelweiss 68
eel 108, 228, 313, 321
   moray 246, 250, 251
   pelican 242
   snipe 243
egret, cattle 144
89 (eighty-nine) butterfly 349
Elephant 140-141
   African 125, 128, 140, 301
   Asian, or Indian 128, 213, 215,
     217, 299
elk, American 75
elytron 346
emu 147, 148, 156, 305, 330
environment 355
environmental degradation 355
environmental impact 355
environmentalism 355
eolian energy 355
Erebus, Mount 27
Ermine 40, 290
European Animals,
     Classifications 290-294
European Forests 92-94
eutrophication 355
Everest, Mount 53, 55
Everglades (swamps) 187
extinction 355

F

falcon, peregrine 104, 291, 334
Famous Animals 360-368
Farm Animals,
     Classifications 308-310
Farmyard Animals 257-282
fat 22, 67
feathers 330
Felix the Cat 363
fennec 171, 173, 300
fer-de-lance 193
fieldfare 332
fieldmouse 61
fin 313
finch, Gouldian 331
firefly 347
Fish 312-325
   clown 245, 246, 251
   elephant-trunk 313, 314

flying 231, 232, 312, 313
   lantern 241
   paradise 314, 315
   parrot, See parrotfish
   pilot 238
   pipe-fish 228
   piranha 315
   porcupine 314, 317
   rabbit-fish 242
   scorpion 228, 249, 315, 316
   tripod 242
   trumpet 316
flamingo 330
flea 347
flicker, northern 85
Flipper 363
Florida 184, 187
fly
   fruit 347
   greenbottle 347, 348
   house 348
   syrphid 346, 350
   tachnid 350
   tsetse 350
flycatcher 337
   pied 334
food chain 355
food web 355
Forests 355
   African 198-201
   Amazon 190-194
   Australian 146-147
   Canadian 74-77
   European 90-94
   South American 190-194
   Temperate 70-71
   The United States 84-86
fossa 211
fossil energy 355
fossil fuels 355
Fox 98
   American gray 85
   arctic 31, **38,** 295
   bat-eared 127, 302
   fennec 171, 173, 300
   kit 179
   red 38, 91, 294
francolin 125
frigate 330
frigatebird 229
fritillary (butterfly) 347
frog 110, 342, 364
   golden poison 193

green 323
Malaysian flying 343
strawberry poison 342, 343
tree 343
fry 313
fulmar 17

G

Gaia 355
gallinule, purple 187
gar, longnose 314, 316
garpike 187
gastropods 347
gaucho 122
gavial 216, 223, 340
Ganges 340, 341
sonda 342
gayal 214, 298
Gazelle 134-135
Dorcas 171
Grant's 134
Mongolian 163
Persian 53
Thomson's 134, 301
gecko 175, 340, 341
Geese of the Campidoglio 364
genet 92, 125, 293
gentian, yellow 62
geothermal energy 356
gerbil, Egyptian 171, 173
gerenuk 135
German shepherd 277
gerrhosaurine 342
gibbon 213
gigantactis 241
gila monster 179
gills 313, 342
Giraffe 112, 125, 128, **136-137,** 301
glider
greater 167
sugar 147, 151, 304
global 356
gnu, brindled 128, 303
Goat 271, 309
Rocky Mountain 45, 46, 75, 285
goby 325
Golden Ass 364
Golden Fish, The 364, 367
goldfinch 326, 330
goldfish 256, 282, 310, 313, 323
Goofy 364

Goose 274, 309, 328, 330, 337
Canada 31, 105
Magellan 49
snow 36, 290
Gorilla 197, 201, **208,** 302
goshawk 330, 333
grasshopper 107, 347
grayling 31, 319
Great Barrier Reef 246
Great Plains of South America 120-121
grebe 331
great-crested 331
red-necked 213
green 356
greenfinch 331, 336
greenhouse effect 356
Greenpeace 356
greyhound, English 279
Grimm, Jakob and Wilhelm 363, 364
Ground Squirrels 33
grouper 250, 251, 314
grouse
black 61, 63
Pallas's sand 163
sage 115, 116
wood 337
guanaco 49, 51
gudgeon 323
guinea fowl 263, 308, 331
vulturine 125
guinea pig 273, 309
gull 20, 229, 331
gunnel, rock 249

H

hammerkop 330, 331
hamster 273, 282
Hare 72, 91, **100-101**
arctic 31
brown 292
Patagonian 123
snowshoe 73, 284
hatchetfish 243
hawfinch 334
hawkmoth, hummingbird 344, 348
health 356
Hedgehog 91, 94, **96-97,** 292
hen 260, 326
herbalists 359
heron 110, 331

great white 187
green-backed 187
squacco 213
Herriot, James 364
hibernation 72
Himalayas 53
hinny 268
hippocampus, See sea horse
Hippopotamus 184, 200, **202-203,** 302
hoatzin 195, 331, 332
hog, pygmy 95, 299
honey 103
hoopoe 329, 337
Hooves and Horns 64-65
hornbill 197, 198, 328, 332, 335
rhinoceros 224, 298, 332
hornet 347
Horns 64-65
Horse 259, 261, **266-267,** 308
Argentine 123
Belgian 267
Caligula's 363
dray 266, 267
Lipizzaner 267
Przewalski's wild 163
steppes 164
Trojan Horse 364, 368
wild 267
horsefly 348, 350
Horus 364
House Pets 282
Huey, Dewey, and Louie 364
hummingbird 192, 332
magnificent 49
sword-billed 195, 289, 331, 336
husky 35, 285
Hydra 364
hydroelectric energy 356
hydroponics 356
hyena 133, 139
hymenoptera 348
hyrax 176

I

ibex, Alpine 61, 64, 65, 291
ibis
scarlet 332, 335
white 187
ice age 46
iguana 341
marine 341

imbalance 356
impala 112, 125, 134, 135, 303
Indian Pachyderms 217
Indios 191
Insects 344-351, 348
Inuit 15
Invertebrates 344-351
Ippogrifo 364

J

jacana 213, 333
  American 326
jackal 175
  black-backed 302
  side-striped 126
jackass, laughing 168
jackdaw 332
jaeger, long-tailed 31, 36, 105
jaguar 191, 194, 289
jaguarundi 121, 122, 288
jellyfish 226, 231
John Dory 250, 313
John the Evangelist 365
Jungle, Amazon 192-194
Asian 212-216

K

kallima inachus 347
Kangaroo 147, 150, **152-153**
  great gray 306
  Lumholtz's tree 151, 153, 305
  rat 168
  red 169
kea 160, 307
kestrel 332
kiang 163
kid 259
Kilimanjaro, Mount 125
killifish 314, 316
King Kong 364
kingfisher 109, 332, 336
Kipling, Rudyard 365
kite 332
kiwi 160, 306, 332
Koala 155, 147, 305
kookaburra, laughing 167, 168
krill 15, 20
kudu
  greater 303
  lesser 125

L

La Fontaine, Jean de 363, 365, 368
Lady and the Tramp 365
ladybug 348
Laika 365, 366
lamb 259, 365
lamprey, river 323
langur 43, 55, 297
lantern fish 241
lapwing 105
lark 107, 332
  horned 115
larva 348
  goldsmith beetle 106
  mole cricket 106
Lassie 277, 365
leaf roller 346, 348
leech 323
Lemmings 17, 31, **33,** 285
lemur 210-211
  black 211
  dwarf 211
  mongoose 211
  ring-tailed 211
leopard 197, 199, 200, 213, 219, 300
  clouded 219
  Snow 53, **57,** 296
lepidopteran 348
Lhasa 43
lice 347
limpets 251
limpkin 187
Lion 112, 125, **132-133,** 300
lionfish 314, 315
litter 356
little owl 330
Little Red Riding Hood 363
lizard 106
  dabb 340
  eggs 106
  frilled 167, 169, 304, 340, 341
  green 107, 340
  horned 179, 340
  monitor 147, 168, 205
  plated 342
  viviparous 342
  wall 342
Llama, 49, **51,** 288
loach
  common 321

spined 321
lobster 251, 254, 255, 314, 316
  European 226, 254
Loch Ness Monster 365, 367
locust 175
London, Jack 362, 365, 366
loon, arctic 31
Lorenz, Konrad 365
lorikeet, rainbow 147
loris, slender 218, 298
Luke the Evangelist 364
lungfish 315
Lynx 71, 75, **82-83**
lyrebird 156, 305

M

macaque, Japanese 71, 297
macaw 333
  blue-and-yellow 195, 289, 333
  green-winged 191
  scarlet 333
mackerel 231
Madagascar 210-211
madrepores 247, 256
magpie
  Chinese 224, 329
  common 329, 333
  green 331
malamute, Alaskan 35
mallard 105, 110, 213, 274, 292, 325, 333
mamba, black 338
mandrill 197
manta ray 226
mantis, praying 107, 349
manul 163
mara 121, 123, 288
marabou 201, 328, 333
  greater 213
marble cone 247
Mark the Evangelist 365
markhor 54, 59, 296
marmoset
  Geoffrey's 191
  silvery 191
Marmot 66-67
  alpine 61, 63, 291
  hoary 75
  yellow-bellied 45
Marshlands 110
Marsupials 150-151, 168
marten 94